Rob Parker changed our org
stewardship, partnership, and
of our workers to get on the fie
hyperbole, we couldn't have done it without Rob.

This book provides the biblical vision and the practical tools for anyone who seeks to serve full-time as a missionary to develop a financial team. I can't promise that you won't feel uncomfortable, but Rob does an excellent job of guiding you to effectively raise financial support and build your team for sustainable growth.

Brian Kim

President, Antioch Center for Training and Sending (ACTS)

Rob Parker's knowledge in partnership is a gift to the Body of Christ and missionaries all over the world. His teaching has been transformational to my life and our missionary community. This book in many ways breaks culture barriers and allows the Word of God to take its rightful place in the area of partnership.

Brian Barcelona

Founder, One Voice Student Missions

This book is a Godsend for missionaries and those in ministry. Get it. Read it. Its message is deeply empowering, extremely encouraging, and thoroughly biblical. A major game changer in the field of missions.

Joel Richardson

New York Times best-selling author, teacher

Among those who send and those who go, there is a tragic lack of clarity on the issue of finances. If we are going to take the Great Commission seriously, we need to take seriously all that the Bible says about how the Lord of the harvest wants to fund it. Rob Parker has done the Body of Christ a great service in writing this book. I heartily commend it.

Dalton Thomas

Founder and Director, Frontier Alliance International

Rob's teaching on biblical partnership is a gift of the Lord to the Body of Yeshua around the world. I saw how well this model works firsthand, proving you don't need to be well known, have a large audience, or promote yourself—just believe that God has a team for you!

Joel
Israel

We were a "normal" family, living out a "normal" American life, when God called us to serve in Uganda. We had no idea how to begin raising financial support. Without Rob's wisdom, which he shares in this book, we would have never made it out of the States. We now live in Uganda, serving orphaned and destitute children. We thank God for the wisdom that He imparted to Rob. Not only did the principles in the book give us practical step-by-step guidelines on how to develop partnership, but they also helped give us a biblical mindset for our finances.

Chad and Sarah Spencer
Founders, Fields of Grace Ministries

Rob Parker has prepared a model of support raising that encompasses the holistic love of Jesus through a paradigm shift toward partnership and away from fundraising. It is good stewardship, and it works. Having taught and deployed this content at Bethany International for three years now, I can confidently say it is life-changing material.

Doug Goodmundson
Director of Development, Bethany International

THE
FULLY FUNDED
MISSIONARY

*A Biblically Based, Hope-Filled Guide to
Raising Financial Support*

ROB PARKER

FORERUNNER
PUBLISHING
KANSAS CITY, MISSOURI

The Fully Funded Missionary by Rob Parker

Published by Forerunner Publishing
International House of Prayer
3535 E. Red Bridge Road
Kansas City, Missouri 64137
ihopkc.org/books

ISBN: 978-1-938060-30-4
eBook ISBN: 978-1-938060-31-1

Edited by Edie Mourey
Cover design by Jared Smith/Wesley Harmon
Interior design by Lala England
Printed in the United States of America

I dedicate this book to all the called, occupational missionaries who haven't known they could work with a partnership team. It is my prayer that you find its pages filled with truth and encouragement and that it serves to inspire and empower you as you serve King Jesus. You are His worker, and you are worthy of a wage.

CONTENTS

Acknowledgments ix

Preface xi

Introduction 1

**Part One:
The Current Landscape**

Chapter One: The Current Crisis in Missions................... 13

Chapter Two: Living Beyond the Myths............................23

**Part Two:
God's Idea of Financial Partnership**

Chapter Three: Biblical Stewardship 37

Chapter Four: Old Testament Pictures
of Partnership 57

Chapter Five: Teamwork in the New Testament 77

Chapter Six: Self-Funding vs. Partnership.......................97

Chapter Seven: Living by Faith Alone?........................... 115

**Part Three:
A Modern Application of Biblical Partnership**

Chapter Eight: A Proven Model
for Partnership Development 135

Chapter Nine: Define Vision...145

Chapter Ten: Prepare for Contact 161

Chapter Eleven: Gather People 177

Chapter Twelve: Share the Vision
& Invite to Partner 195

Part Four:
Expanding & Keeping Our Team

Chapter Thirteen: Extend Our Reach.............................. 217

Chapter Fourteen: Strengthen Our Team
through Yearly Visits 233

Chapter Fifteen: Love Our Team Well..............................249

Chapter Sixteen: We Can Do It! 265

Epilogue 279

Illustrations..281

Notes 299

Bibliography...301

ACKNOWLEDGMENTS

I want to give a special thanks to the people and organizations responsible for shaping my thinking on the subject of partnership development. In addition to the authors mentioned in the bibliography, I am grateful to Cru (formerly known as Campus Crusade for Christ) as it has forged the way in partnership development. Thank you for your leadership in placing so many workers in the mission field. I wish to express my gratitude to Support Raising Solutions (SRS) for your labor of training missionaries in partnership development—because of your work many are serving today.

Doug Goodmundson and Chris Guzzardo, I want to thank you both for the countless hours of conversation whereby you helped to clarify my thoughts regarding partnership development and assisted in the creation of a good training program.

Eunice Cho, thank you for all the time you spent with the notes, training sessions, designs, and administrative work.

David Sluka, you convinced me that I actually had a book— and that I could write it! Without your encouragement, I doubt I would have had the courage to finish.

To my own partnership team, without you I would not have stayed in missions for long. Because of your consistent commitment and encouragement, hundreds of missionaries have been placed in full-time service. Thank you for your partnership in the furtherance of the gospel.

To my wife, Rhonda, I am especially grateful for you. Thank you for all the sacrifice you have made in order for the ministry and this book to go forward. Thank you for accommodating my writing schedule and my fluctuating moods, and for talking me down off the ledge a dozen times. Without you, I would have quit a long time ago.

PREFACE

I had two missionaries in mind when I started writing this book—the veteran who has struggled financially for years and the new missionary not yet active in full-time service because he or she didn't see a financially viable way to move forward. There is a lot that could be said about the rapidly changing world of missions, fundraising, giving trends, and micro business, but because of the two workers I have in mind, I have limited the scope of this work.

Additionally, I had three goals in writing this book: 1) to show that we have a crisis in missions in that we have a lack of workers due to a lack of funding; 2) to identify the truth of God's Word and how He has been funding workers for thousands of years; and 3) to empower laborers with truth and to equip them with practical tools and a plan for moving forward.

In "Part Three: A Modern Application of Biblical Partnership," I start to share the process of how to build a financial partnership team based on the model that we see emerge from the Scriptures. Part 3 points us to a process and outlines the steps for us. The process outlined there should be very helpful in developing missions partners. However, it is not a detailed plan and does not cover everything necessary for building a partnership team. Reading the section will provide assistance in understanding the basic concepts and best practices, but all the nuances of partnership development will not be addressed. For further assistance in partnership development, refer to the website http://www.partnershipdevelopment.org. The site offers courses and additional information. Also available is a companion manual, *Partnership Development for the Fully Funded Missionary*.

Lastly, allow me one more point of clarification. When I use terms like "full-time worker," "full-time ministry," or "called to full-time service," I am referring to the ones who God is asking for a level of service that requires more time and energy from them and, as a result, does not allow for a marketplace job. I believe, in one sense, that every born-again believer is in full-time ministry. We all need to love the people around us, serve our churches, and be good witnesses, and we need to do these things all the time. That being said, I understand God wants some people to do ministry full-time as their occupation/vocation. God draws a few to a level of service and obedience that requires more time and energy than a full-time marketplace job would allow. Jesus was a carpenter by trade, and I am sure He ministered on the job and throughout His life. There was a day and time, though, that His Father required a little more from Him, which led to His transitioning from the carpenter vocation to that of a "full-time" occupational ministry worker.

It doesn't matter to me where we serve—whether at the office, in a school, in our homes, or as a full-time minister. What I care about is that we obey God in our service. One arena is not better than the other. One service is not better than the other. Obedience is the goal, and if we all obey, God is glorified.

A Collaborative Effort

God is into collaboration. As hard as it may be to believe, He doesn't enjoy working alone. He's looking for partners. He could have chosen any number of ways, for example, to financially supply His workers on the mission field, but He chose the giving of the saints as the primary means. He is looking for men and women who will agree with His purpose and mission, who will agree with the people He's using to do His mission, and who will agree with the personal role He wants them to play within it.

What is God's ultimate goal? He desires to advance and build His kingdom as He redeems and restores the earth. And His method is to do so *with us* as we agree *with Him* in His work.

The giving and stewardship of God's people advance almost every aspect of Christian ministry. Churches, missions, Christian schools, and parachurch organizations are almost completely funded, the majority of the time, by God's people. Even when ministries are funded by sales, those sales are most often from Christian products or Christian services purchased by Christians.

What we can infer from these things, then, is God's building plan requires partnership: people partnering with people and people partnering with God. Such collaboration requires us to willingly and fully submit to Him and to one another as good stewards throughout the entire process. So when we invite people to partner with us in ministry, we simply are giving them an opportunity to partner with God, steward His resources, advance His mission, and build His kingdom in the earth. But that's not how every believer sees it.

A Conversion in Our Thinking

Few people, if any, enter occupational ministry because they like to raise money. However, most of those individuals quickly discover that partnership development is essential to fully complete their assignment and to do so with longevity. The bottom line is, they cannot fulfill the call of God on their lives without the resources to sustain that call. Obedience to the call has a price tag attached to it, after all.

Currently, in most mission circles, there is an aversion to asking about financial partnership for a variety of reasons. Most people would rather not deal with the subject at all. They often fear rejection, think they don't have biblical permission to ask for finances, or believe missionaries are supposed to be poor. Several organizations do not even allow their missionaries to raise support at all, believing it is contrary to faith.

I believe almost all fear, disagreement, or hesitation around the subject of raising support is rooted in our culture—not in the kingdom of God. When I say, "our culture," I am referring to our Western church culture. Popular yet erroneous teaching about personal finances, missions giving and support, and the role of faith in it all has been preached and promoted, creating a real bias against raising support. And it is this cultural stronghold that often keeps us from even starting the process necessary to fulfill our call.

The number one hindrance to successful partnership development lies between our ears. To be successful in partnership development, we must first have a paradigm shift from a *cultural mindset* to a *biblical mindset*. Our current cultural mindset is driven by fear, lack of understanding, opinion, "mammon," and tradition. It has sidelined thousands of workers, leaving their assignments largely undone, and has negatively impacted global missions as a result.

As I look to God's Word on the subject, I see something that has not only been overlooked but even denied at times by fellow Christians. Scripture presents a culture of partnership: the saints work together as they join God's will for the earth. And that work includes the financing of the same.

The Bible has much to say about workers and their wages, the Church's commission in these last days, the stewardship of every believer, and the rewards of giving. It's clear that God's desire is for the Body of Christ to be submitted to Him and to one another as we work together in humility and as we partner together for His kingdom.

The Language of Partnership Development

We need to shift our thinking from being culturally based to being biblically based. When we make this shift, our language should change as well. Additionally, we need to shift the discussion from *fundraising* to *biblical partnership*. Fundraising has its place in our current culture, but partnership is very different, and it is the focus of this book.

If a worker feels *forced* into fundraising because of financial needs, the whole process is often negative for everyone involved; ergo, fundraising becomes "a necessary evil." On the other hand, if the worker becomes involved in *partnership development* as a ministry to the Body of Christ, then the journey can be both fulfilling and fruitful. Comparing these different mindsets helps us distinguish between fundraising and biblical partnership (see chart below).

Fundraising	Biblical Partnership
Unpleasant and difficult	Positive (ministry)
Transactional	Transformational
Technique	Body of Christ in relationship
Donor	Partner
Donate	Invest
Short-term	Long-term
Need-focused	Vision-focused
Pressure to give (sales)	Invitation to join God

As you can see, there are several differences between these two approaches to financing a God-given vision. When we walk in biblical partnership, which is the family of God working together, it imparts life to the heart of the goer and the sender, and makes God smile. Partnership is a lifestyle that focuses on relationship and is a joy-filled ministry to God's people, helping them to connect with the Great Commission and grow in their generosity. Fundraising, on the other hand, focuses on raising money, doesn't have to be relational, and often becomes the dreaded yearly event that everyone hates. Where fundraising is all about the transaction and the technique used to secure a donor and receive a donation, biblical partnership is all about ministry and relationship and the family of God working together to fulfill His mandate. It's more than transactional, then; it's transformational. And because of this, the outcome is long-term support by the partner and long-term service by the missionary versus the short-term support and service fundraising supplies.

Biblical partnership is God's designed way to fund His workers and His mission in the earth today. When we partner with God in the way He has ordained, there are tremendous benefits in raising a team who partners with us in the ministry assignment He has given us.

Benefits of Raising a Team

Building a partnership team can be one of the most satisfying experiences we will ever have. Helping other Christians realize how they can be part of a team that is making an impact for the kingdom of God is exhilarating. When we understand we are not simply asking for monies for ourselves but for a vision the Lord has called us to do, we distance ourselves from the "hat-in-hand" beggarly image often associated with raising support. Instead, we are able to see ourselves as asking on His behalf and asking for His purposes. And by raising a team to partner with us, we will be providing members of the Body of Christ a stewardship opportunity to give to that work.

Being properly funded will strengthen our mission organizations and, therefore, strengthen the missions' movement. In fact, we will be providing opportunities for the Body of Christ to participate in God's global mission. Furthermore, it will also help us build a prayer base for our ministries, as well as build a number of relationships that would not have developed otherwise.

While gathering partners, we are engaged in real ministry to God's people. We are building relationships; in fact, the kingdom is all about relationships. So partnership development is not something we do in order to be in ministry; rather, it is ministry.

It is critical to understand that partnership development is not a means to an end but is actually a key part of our God-given assignment. Because developing partners is part of our ministry, we prepare our hearts with the same intensity as we do for any other aspect of ministry. And we prepare our materials, invitations, and sharing points with as much prayer, diligence, and practice as we do for preaching, church planting, or discipleship ministry.

Key Ingredients of Successful Partnership Development

There are four key ingredients to successful partnership ministry. They are faith, strategy, diligence, and improvisation.

FAITH IN GOD

Successful partnership development starts with the revelation that God is the One who meets *all* our needs, even while He requires us to work hard. Hard work is our act of faith, trusting God to honor and bless the labor of our hands and bring His provision into our lives. Having faith means rising above discouragement, being sure of our calling, and believing God at all times, no matter what the circumstances are saying. If God has called us and partnership is His preferred way, then He must have a team for us to partner with.

A STRATEGIC PLAN

God is a visionary, and because we are created in God's image, He has given us the gift of vision as well. Our hearts are stirred by vision. But vision alone is not enough; every vision must have a strategy attached to it.

"If you fail to plan, you plan to fail. If you aim at nothing, you are sure to hit it." We have heard these or similar business commentary before, and they are true, even for us believers. The fact is, after all, that fulfilling the calling and assignment of God won't *just happen* on its own. We must have a strategy for success. This is why the writer of Proverbs says, "The *plans* of the diligent lead surely to *abundance*, but everyone who is hasty comes only to poverty" (Prov. 21:5 ESV).

DILIGENCE

Those who succeed in partnership development are those who know how to keep themselves on track. They are individuals who push themselves when they do not feel like making a phone call or typing out a letter. Partnership development is a time-intensive ministry that requires we stick to the plan, make commitments to core concepts, and faithfully walk out best practices every day. Without the diligence to do so, we might come up short in the plans and vision that God has put in our hearts.

IMPROVISATION

Sometimes life, work, and schedules get in the way and make it difficult for us to reach our potential partners. In this book, I will provide a clear model and the steps to follow, but be aware that we must be willing to improvise and determine within ourselves to have an overcoming, *can-do* attitude. While being careful to stick with the important concepts of partnership development, we often have to move into plan B and do the plan on the fly.

Developing a partnership team will challenge us to grow as Christians. If we are faithful, strategic, diligent, and willing to improvise, it will be an incredibly formative and maturing process for us.

A Vision of Cookie Jars

I knew the Lord had called me to missions, and the season had come for me to make the transition. My wife and I had said *yes*, but I was unsure how it would financially work. After twenty years in the marketplace, I wasn't sure what to do about an income for missions. Was it by faith, and if it was, what did that even mean? Was I supposed to be poor? Was I to build a webpage and advertise myself? I didn't know what to do.

One early morning, I was outside on my front porch, praying and asking God these questions about money. Suddenly, I found myself in the middle of some sort of dream or vision. In this state, I was in my three-storied house, which was packed full of cookie jars. Yes, I just said cookie jars. They were everywhere— every horizontal surface was covered with them. I bent down and opened a jar, and to my surprise, I found a small handful of money. I quickly opened another jar, which was empty, and another jar, which was also empty. I reached for another, and instead of being empty, it had a handful of change. After a couple more empty jars, I reached for another. When I opened this last jar, I pulled out a large handful of cash.

Holding this newfound money in my hand, I looked around at the hundreds and hundreds of jars that I had not yet opened. Then quietly I heard the Lord whisper in my spirit, "I have money stashed in vessels all over town. Your job is to go lift the lid." As suddenly as this experience began, it was over, and I was back on my front porch. The message was clear; I knew the Lord wanted me to look into support raising.

Lifting the Lid

This book is the result of my pursuing the Lord and His Word regarding going and lifting the lid. I have learned that it's all about relationship and partnering together for the advancement of our Father's kingdom. And my desire with this book is to share how to forge such relationships in obedience to God's Word. In the end, I trust the freedom to pursue God's calling to the harvest-ready fields will be enabled by great team building.

The book itself is divided into four parts. In Part One, I present the current problem that exists in missions. Part Two demonstrates how financial partnership is God's idea; it's how we can "fix" the problem. Part Three provides a modern-day application to building a partnership team to accomplish individual assignments. And Part Four sheds light on expanding and keeping a team.

To further assist in understanding and applying the information, a section titled, "Looking Inside," and one called, "Taking Action," are included. The former helps us interact thoughtfully and introspectively with the text, while the latter sends us out to do something related to what we have read.

To those of us who are on the journey of partnership development, this book should be a good reminder that none of us can fulfill the call of God alone. We need others to help us along the way. God has established partnership as His preferred method of funding His mission in the earth today. And God has a team who wants to partner with us to help us fulfill the call of God on our lives.

PART ONE:
THE CURRENT LANDSCAPE

The first step to overcoming a problem is admitting there is one. We have a problem in missions. Even though God is doing amazing things in almost every corner of the earth, the world of missions is greatly understaffed and underfunded. Of the entire full-time missionary workforce, less than 4 percent is working in the 10/40 window, where 88 percent of the world's unreached people live. And of all the money that North America sows into missions, only five cents of every hundred dollars goes to the 10/40 window.

With such a clear command from Scripture to go into all the world and make disciples, and with such a clear need in the 10/40 window, why are so few working there? And why are they so poorly funded? In this first section, we are going to look at the current situation in missions, its root cause, and how to overcome it.

CHAPTER ONE

The Current Crisis in Missions

Thoughts have consequences.

The Need Today

God is doing great things around the world today in missions. He is calling and sending missionaries into some of the hardest parts of the world to effectively reach people with the good news of the gospel of Christ. Yet, the field of missions is facing a crisis. In the 10/40 window at the moment of this book's publication, the ratio between gospel worker and the lost is about 225,000 to 1. The greatest need today is the same as when Jesus mentioned it two thousand years ago—more available workers (see Mt. 9:36–38).

The full-time workers I have come into contact with are some of the most amazing people I have ever met. I'm absolutely surprised, stunned, and blessed by the lives my friends lead. They repeatedly give, serve, and labor—being compelled by the love of God. Countless times they have exchanged the visible, easier, more profitable and prestigious high road for the hidden, often hard, modest, occupationally-damaging low road of humility and meekness, just to remain at the feet of Jesus a little while longer. I am often overwhelmed by a profound sense of privilege as I look around at the collection of people among whom the Lord has set me.

From what I have seen, though, many missionaries serve God from a place of financial weakness rather than strength. It is disheartening to see these incredible, called, gifted, and humble servants leave their field of service over the issue of consistent lack of funding. I have seen missionaries come and go—often within a couple of years—due to a lack of financial support. Many divine assignments have come to a screeching halt because there wasn't enough money to continue on.

I'm not talking about people who have prematurely jumped into ministry here, operating out of enthusiasm more than a divine call. Rather, I'm talking about men and women who have divine assignments on their lives, have heard the Lord in the right timing, have sought biblical counsel, and have moved into ministry under His leadership. I have seen a number of my friends go through intense, emotional struggles over the lack of finances, often questioning their calling and even God, and occasionally getting upset with people they thought should support their work. And that's not all! Their marriages and families have evidenced a great deal of strain and stress resulting from their situation.

If workers remain in this state for too long, a number of negative thoughts and behaviors begin to manifest in their lives. Consistent lack will cause individuals to make decisions they would not normally make. Often, they will resort to secular techniques in their ministry, such as heavy-handed marketing, pushy sales, or faulty promises of blessing—each of which wields an unbiblical pressure to give to their cause. All of this is bad for the Body of Christ and has a negative impact on the mission of the Church.

Where Are All the Workers?

According to most estimates, there are about four hundred thousand full-time, occupational missionaries working around the world today, which does not include pastors or church staff. The number may be as high as six hundred thousand if we also consider the few thousand unknown cases of missionaries in poor regions, where there is no record of their work. For the sake of ease, let's assume that there are a lot more than we know and round the number up to one million non-church staff missionaries working on our planet today.

There are about seven billion people on the earth, with about five hundred and fifty million of them born-again Christians, which means there are about five hundred and fifty million believing Christians called by Jesus to do the work of reaching the other six and a half billion unbelieving people. Does the number of occupational missionaries (one million) in relation to the number of professing Christians (550 million) sound right? If we do the math, we find that only about one-fifth of 1 percent of the Body of Christ is presently engaged in occupational missions.

If only 1 percent of the Body of Christ were called into full-time missions work, that would be five million workers, which is slightly more than ten times the number we currently see. Let's say only half of 1 percent of the Body of Christ is called to the mission field: that would still mean two and a half million missionaries, which is five times more than we are now seeing in active service. I do not believe that half of 1 percent, or even 1 percent, is the *real* number of Christians God has called into full-time missions work. The percentages should be much higher.

It is my belief that there are a few million Christians called to the mission field who are not active in full-time missions. I see this group of people far too often, people with a call of God upon their lives yet they have given their lives to something else entirely. When I talk to them, their response is typically the same: "I would love to go into full-time missions, but I just don't see how I can financially make that happen." People feel a pull toward missions, and they do the only thing they know how to do: raise just enough money for one short trip or finance a trip on their own.

Please do not misunderstand me here. I thank the Lord for the missionaries who are in the field, and I thank the Lord for short-term mission trips that almost anyone can take. Many people have come into the kingdom through these trips. Even though God works through these, I do believe more believers are called than are presently involved in active service, and again, I believe the number is in the millions. I think a major reason for their inactivity—if not *the* main reason—is the issue of financial support.

Not answering the money question can keep us from going; it also can keep us from staying long-term in our field of service. I was having a conversation with a missionary who had been serving full-time for about eight years. He informed me that he was leaving missions due to a lack of funding and felt as though the

Lord was leading him back to the marketplace. Immediately, red flags were popping up in my mind as I thought to myself, *Is God leading you back to the marketplace, or are you broke and interpreting it as the Lord leading you back?* Then he said something that pains me every time I hear it. He said, "The money has dried up . . . the grace has lifted."

Sensing that he was still called to missions, I asked him this question, "If I could show you how to raise $2,500 dollars a month in a way that imparted life to your heart and made Jesus smile, would you stay in missions?"

Quickly and excitedly, he said, "Yes, absolutely!"

He didn't realize what he had said, but his words revealed that his lack was causing him to misinterpret what the Lord was saying. Once I solved his money problem, suddenly his calling was to stay in missions.

Jesus said, "The harvest truly is plentiful, but the laborers are few. Therefore pray the Lord of the harvest to send out laborers into His harvest" (Mt. 9:37–38). In Jesus' time, the need was for more workers, not for the harvest to have more time to ripen. The need was the same then as it is now: the Great Commission needs a fully available, fully equipped, and properly empowered workforce. Jesus didn't highlight a lack of funds as the problem; He pointed to the lack of available people who would go. How can this be? If they are called and they are obeying the Lord, the funding should be there, right?

Yes, it should. So why are so many called men and women leaving the mission field, or never going into the field to begin with? Again, it is due mostly to perspective and attitude regarding funding.

The Stronghold that Possesses Our Minds

As we discussed in our introduction, there is a large and powerful stronghold in the minds of those within the Church. I believe it either contributes to or is directly responsible for about 95 percent of our unbiblical thinking concerning giving and partnership in the harvest. Much of this unbiblical thinking is expressed in various excuses.

When I talk to people about the idea of raising support, I hear anything from their need to work a "real job" to their need to "make tents." In their minds, this is how they should fund their missionary endeavors, meaning they need to have some sort of legitimate job and then minister on the side. Some even suggest that it is a lack of faith to raise funds before going onto the mission field.

Again, this all seems rooted in fear, shame, and unbelief. Rather than being shaped by the Word of God, we are all too often shaped by our culture. It is very important that Scripture shapes our worldview when we talk about funding and missions—nothing else.

When I say, "stronghold," what exactly am I talking about? Paul wrote to the Corinthians, admonishing them to demolish the strongholds that had been set up in their minds and were contrary to the thoughts of God. Paul said:

For though we walk in the flesh, we are not waging war according to the flesh. For the weapons of our warfare are not of the flesh but have divine power to destroy strongholds. We destroy arguments and every lofty opinion raised against the knowledge of God, and take every thought captive to obey Christ. (2 Cor. 10:3–5 ESV).

The strongholds indicated here are arguments and lofty opinions raised against the knowledge of God—meaning of who He is and what He has revealed Himself to be throughout biblical history. It is easy to get the impression from these verses that strongholds are always bad, meaning they are negative strongholds. And, in a sense, the strongholds Paul told us to demolish are of the negative kind because they stand against who God has revealed Himself to be.

However, the Bible uses words like *refuge, strong tower,* and *fortress* to describe positive strongholds as well (see Ps. 9:9; 18:2; 37:39). From these few references, we can see that the stronghold itself is neither positive nor negative. In fact, what makes a stronghold negative or positive are the ones building the stronghold and their intended purpose in building it.

In the natural, a stronghold is a fortified place, a fortress (like a castle or walled city), a place for survival or refuge, or a place chosen for strategic military purposes. Strongholds, when spoken of in this context, are fortified places that are mainly built in the mind. Simply put, strongholds are a collection of thoughts that are built when we repeatedly agree with *truth* or *lies.* Our thoughts, as we know, lead to our attitude, and our attitude leads to action.

The strongholds we are fighting regarding funding and missions (i.e., "I need to be a tent maker," "I need to have a legitimate job," etc.) are not righteous, Scripture does not shape them, and they are not submitted to the lordship of Christ. Later, I'll address Paul's tent making, but for our purposes here, we need to see that the provision of monies from our own labor to go and labor for God is not a scriptural requirement. It's not the "righteous" thing to do. This thinking, then, is a stronghold that is not of God. Having it and keeping it will result in wrong attitudes and inaction or the wrong action.

In Second Corinthians, Paul is stating that the spiritual warfare we are fighting is against negative strongholds of the mind. Every believer faces a spiritual battle on a daily basis that *begins* and *ends* with the thought patterns of our minds. That is why Paul emphasized the importance of Christians renewing their minds with the truth of God's Word in order to avoid being conformed to this world: "Do not be conformed to this world, but be transformed by the renewal of your mind, that by testing you may discern what is the will of God, what is good and acceptable and perfect" (Rom. 12:2 ESV).

By agreeing with something not supported in God's Word, we in essence are agreeing with someone or something else. In this case, I believe we end up agreeing with the enemy because it is he who does not want God's mission accomplished in the earth. And if we allow him to build a stronghold of lies in our minds, then we develop an ungodly or worldly mindset, which in turn leads to bad behavior patterns. Every time we agree with a demonic lie, we help the kingdom of darkness build a stronghold in our own minds. Fifteen years later, what seemed like an insignificant lie has become a huge fortress that is hard to penetrate. Ultimately, we give authority to what we agree with.

Once the Holy Spirit exposes a lie in our minds, however, it is crucial that we break our agreement with that lie. We do this by asking the Holy Spirit to show us the truth, and then we want to quickly agree with His truth. By agreeing with the Holy Spirit, we allow Him to build up a stronghold of truth in our minds, which leads to a right perspective, a holy attitude, and, finally, our obedience.

We are creatures of habit and tend to repeat patterns that are familiar to us, leading to our not wanting to give up our old thought patterns. However, we must allow God's Word to shape our thinking and form our attitudes. We must have our minds renewed by saturating ourselves with the truth of His Word.

Conclusion

Due to a lack of funding, many people who once said yes to Jesus are no longer walking in their calling. Because of the strongholds that abound in the Church, myths have been created that keep us from obeying the Great Commission. Casting down these strongholds and receiving deliverance from wrong thinking are essential to being successful in partnership development. The negative strongholds we have built must be torn down by renewing our minds with the truth of God's Word. The Word of God, and not our culture or the circumstances surrounding us, must shape our worldview.

Looking Inside

- Do you have any wrong thoughts concerning money and funding for missions? (Keep asking yourself this question throughout the book.)
- Have you held back from full-time ministry because of a concern over finances?
- Do you have assignments from the Lord that are not currently being done due to financial lack?
- Is God calling you into missions and possibly the 10/40 window?

Taking Action

1. Take thirty minutes to one hour and do a little research on these websites:
   - Thetravelingteam.org
   - Globalfrontiermissions.org
   - Oneworldmissions.com
   - Frontierventures.org
   - Globalmissionnetwork.info
2. Become familiar with the current situation in missions. Then spend ten minutes a day for the next week praying and talking with the Lord, asking Him if you are to be part of the solution. Write down what you feel the Lord speaks to you.

Consider reading a great book that will help you understand the focal point of missions. I recommend *Let the Nations Be Glad* by John Piper.

CHAPTER TWO

Living Beyond the Myths

There's a solution to the missions problem.
The truth will set us free.

Myths Abound

Unfortunately, the missions movement has a number of myths concerning support raising and the lifestyle that accompanies it.[1] Opinions and ideologies abound. A few have some wisdom, but most are harmful, causing many misunderstandings and unnecessary hardship.

Funding is not the problem with missionaries being sent out. Rather, the problem is a lack of biblical understanding of how to find, gather, and receive those funds. Many missionaries know that "God will provide," but very few understand the biblical pattern of how God does the providing. This lack of understanding is a main reason for many never going into missions or not staying in missions long-term. This is where we need right teaching and good instruction.

In the many years that I have been a believer, I have heard a cautionary statement made several times, usually from an older, wiser Christian to a younger, fiery praying, meditating, fasting Christian. It goes something like this: "Don't be so heavenly minded that you're of no earthly good." There are a number of things wrong with this statement. After all, the reverse of that statement is the true caution, "Don't be so earthly minded that you're of no spiritual good." In all my years, I have never met a person whose mind was fixed on things above yet was of no use to people here on earth. Such a person is a myth; he or she doesn't exist. But the myth has a degree of power. It can talk people out of being fixed on things above.

In our endeavoring to understand what we need to do, let's specifically address some of the myths that have prevented many from moving into raising support and fulfilling their calling. I have seen seven myths or strongholds that are common to people who are considering raising money for missions. They are best expressed through the following statements:

1. "I don't know enough people who will give."
2. "I'm not sure I have enough faith to live on support."
3. "I shouldn't ask for money; I should just pray."
4. "I will never be able to raise enough money to live on."
5. "Raising support is contrary to faith."
6. "If I raise support, I will be broke all the time."
7. "Raising support is unbiblical."

Let's take a look at each of these myths and begin to expose them to the truth.

MYTH 1: NOT KNOWING ENOUGH PEOPLE

The first myth I have heard goes something like this, "I don't know enough people who will give." Even though this is a common myth, the truth is that we know enough people who can support us. Most people actually know somewhere between two hundred and fifty and four hundred people. (This doesn't include the number of people that they are going to meet during the partnership development process.) Granted, most of those we know will never give to missions, but we have a lot of people we can share our vision with and a lot of people who will pray for us. Though many people may not immediately come to mind, the list grows pretty quickly once we write down the names of those we know. Besides, the longer we live, the larger that list can become.

MYTH 2: NOT HAVING ENOUGH FAITH

"I'm not sure I have enough faith to live on support" is the second myth. To do justice to this subject, I will address it more at length in a later chapter. But for now, the fact is we have had enough faith to respond to the call of God on our lives. We have had enough faith to pray for the sick, to witness, and to trust God for food, rent, tuition, and so forth—the basic necessities of life. The faith required to live with support on the mission field is the same faith we are exercising every day in our lives for our basic needs and the advancement of the gospel.

MYTH 3: NOT ASKING FOR MONEY BUT PRAYING INSTEAD

When someone thinks, *I shouldn't ask for money; I should just pray*, it is actually the stronghold talking to them. Asking is biblical, as I will demonstrate later on in this book. Jesus has been promised the nations, yet even He has to ask for them (see Ps. 2:8).

Praying is asking. Praying is essentially agreeing with what the Lord wants to do in and through us. Giving to fund a worker is a little like prayer in that it is agreeing with what God wants to do. He wants to provide for us, and He wants to do it through His people. Asking becomes easier when we see that we are not asking for ourselves but asking for God and others.

MYTH 4: NOT BEING ABLE TO RAISE ENOUGH MONEY

This myth's voice says, "I will never be able to raise enough to live on." To that, I want to respond, "According to my best estimates there are about 250,000 missionaries on the earth right now who are working with support teams. I have met a few thousand of them myself, heard the testimonies of those I have met, and even was involved in their training. One look at well-known missions organizations around the world will bear this out. Many missionaries have families, homes, insurance, retirement, and other similar things requiring good supply." In other words, I want to say, "Other people are able to, so why can't we?"

I personally have been working with a financial partnership team since 2006. It is possible to raise enough money to live on, and to live according to a normal standard of living. Being a missionary doesn't mean we have to be in constant lack. We can have enough.

MYTH 5: NOT RAISING SUPPORT BECAUSE IT'S CONTRARY TO FAITH

Yes, there are those who say that raising support is contrary to faith. As we mentioned before, the issue of faith is possibly the largest stronghold to overcome. Raising support is not contrary to faith; rather, it is faith in action. It takes faith to believe God and step out and share our vision with those we know. Raising support is possibly one of the greatest steps of faith I have ever taken in my own life. Not only that, but partnership development continues to build my faith on an ongoing basis.

MYTH 6: NOT RAISING SUPPORT BECAUSE IT MEANS LIVING IN POVERTY

I have heard individuals say, "If I raise support, I will be broke all the time." They assume they will never be able to raise enough, or they feel missionaries are supposed to be poor. I call this *poor talk* or a *poverty mindset*. When we have a poverty mindset, we focus on our lack, on what we don't have, instead of on what we do have and what God can provide for us. We must take these wrong thoughts captive, submit them to God, and renew our minds with His Word.

The truth is poverty mindsets have been around for a long time. The idea that a Christian, and most definitely a missionary, should be poor and suffer has been pushed by the devil and his cohorts for centuries. We must understand that God has nothing to gain by keeping His servants impoverished. It surely doesn't make Him look like the great provider that He is.

MYTH 7: NOT RAISING SUPPORT BECAUSE IT'S UNBIBLICAL

To those who say raising support is not biblical, I want to know where it says in the Bible we are not to do so. I am confident Scripture does not say that. To the contrary, raising support is *very* biblical. There are about a dozen verses in the New Testament alone that speak directly about financial support and people who are supported by others as they engage in missions. We all understand that it takes money to build the kingdom of God, because ministries have to be funded. Support raising is really just a thoughtful way to go about gathering those funds.

As we go on to discuss raising support from a biblical perspective, we will see a pattern begin to develop. We will then use this scriptural pattern as an outline to our approach, which will be based on what we see in the Word and *not* what we see on Wall Street. Partnership development is not "sales," although I do have to admit that much of what I see going on in the arena of support-raising circles smacks more of sales, business, and marketing than it does the kingdom of God. Allow me to reiterate this point: partnership development is God's way; it's His method of funding His mission.

Partnership in Action

Now that we have looked at the myths that abound, let's see the other side of partnership development. We will go on to develop a biblical model of partnership and raising support, but for now let's just look at the truth of partnership development being God's way to support missionaries throughout the world.

FACT 1: THOUSANDS ALREADY PARTNERING

Presently, there are about a quarter of a million known missionaries on the planet in full-time ministry who are funded through partnership. There should be more, and I believe that there will be. But the existence of these many thousands is proof that partnership clearly works. What we are attempting to do is nothing new or unique; the Lord has been supporting full-time workers through the giving of the saints for thousands of years.

FACT 2: THE NECESSITY OF GIVING

We all need to give. The ministry of partnership development is providing opportunities for God's people to become involved in God's work. Partnership development helps the Christian/steward answer the all-important question, "What do I do with what God has entrusted to me?" And the answer to that question is to give. Giving is a necessity for God's people.

FACT 3: ACCOMPLISHING SOMETHING TOGETHER

Partnership development is an invitation to be part of a team and to accomplish something that can't be done alone. God determined that the funding of His work was to be done through the giving of His people. He has always done it this way, and it is the way He will continue to do it. A *yes* from potential partners is really a statement in which they are saying *yes* to God's ways and will for their lives, as well as helping us fulfill the call of God on our own lives. Partnership is simply agreeing with God; it's doing something together with Him and others. The Body of Christ is a spiritual family, and the family business is missions.

FACT 4: BUILDING TEAMS

Partnership development is building financial partnership teams, not fundraising. In fundraising, once the donation has been made, the transaction is done. In contrast, we are building teams that will work together for years to build the Lord's kingdom. Partnership development is an ongoing relationship of trust and mutual encouragement. Both parties have equal parts to play. A team will always outwork the individual.

FACT 5: MINISTERING TO PEOPLE

Partnership development is a vital aspect of ministry. It *is* ministry to the Body of Christ, *not* what we have to do in order to get into ministry. We will find numerous opportunities to walk in Jesus' second greatest commandment: to love our neighbors as ourselves. Our partners are real people whom the Lord has stirred to join with us in ministry. He *added* them to our partnership team; they are not just a source of income. We must minister to them and love them well.

FACT 6: TESTIFYING OF GOD'S FAITHFULNESS

Partnership development is a testimony of God's faithfulness. Walking into the homes or places of business of others and walking out with their partnership, trust, and friendship is a true act of God. God loves biblical partnership, which evidences His children working together with Him. It is a sign of spiritual health, not a lack of faith.

FACT 7: HAVING THE TIME

We have time for partnership development. God has given us all the time we need to do all that He's called us to do. We will always make time for those things that hold highest priority in our lives. Our other ministry responsibilities are important, but without partnership development we may not stay in ministry long-term. If we don't schedule our time, someone or something else will.

FACT 8: INCLUDING EVERYONE

Everyone is a potential partner, so we need to open up our thinking. God will connect us with all kinds of people from all different backgrounds. Some we will have a history with, and others we may have just met. We may have great relationships with some and have good but not a depth of relationship with others. Relationship is not a prerequisite for asking, but it is necessary for a continued, long-term partnership to be sustained. We may run out of family and friends to partner with us, but we will never run out of people to invite into partnership.

FACT 9: GIVING AGAIN AND AGAIN

People who give are more likely to give again. God is always stirring people and has created them to be stewards of the resources He has given to them. We should keep people informed about all that God is doing through our ministry and give them recurring opportunities to join us in our assignment. We shouldn't worry, for if we love them well, we won't wear them out.

Conclusion

When it comes to raising support, 90 percent of it is perspective. Without the proper perspective regarding this issue, we will not enter into the process with any clarity, confidence, or conviction. A wrong perspective about money is one of the reasons many never enter into full-time ministry in the first place. They feel called by God and have a burden to go, but they just can't see how it is going to financially work out for them.

God didn't stir us inside and call us out into full-time occupational service to have us fail. God knew our circumstances, our families, and culture when He drew us into missions. There is a way to develop the necessary support, and it is a good and healthy God-ordained way. And it is the means to help overcome the crisis in missions.

Looking Inside

- Do you have any mythical thinking about financial support and your situation? (Keep asking yourself this question throughout the book.)

- Are myths keeping you from taking action?

- Myths can cause fear, shame, and guilt. Do you feel afraid, ashamed, or guilty regarding partnership development?

- Do you believe God is bigger than your circumstances?

- Do you believe He has a team for you somewhere?

Taking Action

1. Take about fifteen to twenty minutes a day to sit down with pen and paper and write out the facts—write out what you know for sure about God's call on your life. Don't let the "what ifs" and "what abouts" interfere. You don't have to answer those questions right now. Instead ask yourself:

   - What do I know for sure?

   - What has God placed in me?

   - What has He spoken to me?

   - What are my spiritual gifts?

   - What are my natural talents?

   - Who has He connected me with?

2. Spend a few minutes praying about what you wrote down in your first action step. Do this for four or five days in a row. Then write down any words of encouragement or direction you receive during your prayer time.

PART TWO:
GOD'S IDEA OF
FINANCIAL PARTNERSHIP

Through the ages, God has been consistently financing His global mission. From the abundance of His storehouses and the stewardship of His children, He has empowered, equipped, and sustained those He has called to work with and for Him. He has bankrolled building projects, offerings for the poor, housing for the homeless, and the funding of full-time occupational ministers. When believers give what God has entrusted to them, in the way that God wants them to give, then God's mission goes forward with strength. God's family business is missions, and we are most happy when we serve Him in it.

In this section, we are going to look at the stewardship responsibility God has given to every believer, as well as the recorded history of saints funding workers and the mission of God throughout the earth. We will start to see the brilliant leadership of God in including the voluntary giving of the saints and thus their agreement as a requisite for His restoration plan.

Lastly, there are two common misunderstandings about underwriting missionaries. These have had a negative impact on the Great Commission. They have been the source of much confusion, emotional pain, and unnecessary hardship. We want to gain clarity on these two points, have our minds renewed by the Word of God, and move forward with the confidence and strength of Scripture.

CHAPTER THREE

Biblical Stewardship

Stewardship—it brings significance to the mundane of life, satisfies the soul, affords the opportunity to be great in God, and is the basis of the Christian life.

The psalmist Asaph said God declared that the entire world is His—"and all its fullness"—including the beasts of the forest and the field, and "the cattle on a thousand hills" (Ps. 50:10–12, 24:1). Later on in Scripture, we read that God said the silver and the gold were also His (Hag. 2:8). In short, God owns it all! He said, "It's all mine!" And so it is.

Though God owns the world in its entirety, He graciously grants humanity the privilege and responsibility of managing His workmanship, keeping His creation, and serving within His household. When servants act in love-filled obedience to their Master, that action is called stewardship. It is the biblical basis for living life skillfully and is the lifelong responsibility of every Christian, regardless of his or her occupation. There is considerable dignity in possessing the role of a steward or the position as God's manager. No matter our role in everyday life—business owner, housewife, teacher, lawyer, or construction worker—we all become co-laborers with God when we have the perspective of stewardship and live as servants under His leadership.

Since God is the King who is enthroned, ruling and reigning over all of His creation, then our stewardship simply flows out of His ownership. Our stewardship responsibility before the Lord touches every facet of our lives, not just the financial realm. In fact, it is the foundation for the Christian life. Good stewards simply acknowledge God as Owner, trust Him as Provider, and faithfully manage all that He entrusts to them for His glory.

Stewardship is the responsible management of another's wealth, possessions, and property. It includes thoughtful care, similar to a shepherd to his sheep or the raising of someone else's children. In the Bible, another name for a steward is an overseer or household manager. Five examples from Scripture come to mind:

1. Abraham had a household servant by the name of Eliezer of Damascus. He would have been responsible for overseeing all of the servants, and their daily tasks, and handling Abraham's personal errands. At one point, he had the responsibility of finding a wife for Isaac.

2. Jacob served as the household manager for Laban, even though Laban had used trickery and deceit against him (Gen. 29-31). He kept his flocks among other things.

3. Joseph, after his release from prison, was a household manager for Potiphar. He would have lived in Potiphar's house and run his household. In Genesis 42:6, when Joseph was made governor over the land, he had his own household manager (Gen. 44:1, 4).

4. The household steward, in the parable of the workers in the vineyard, had the responsibility of paying the workers at the end of the day (Mt. 20:8).

5. Chuza, Herod's household manager and husband of Joanna who traveled with Jesus, is mentioned in Luke 8:3.

In actuality, stewardship is walking out the great commandment to love God with all of our heart, soul, mind, and strength. Good stewardship has its rewards as we read regarding Joseph's service:

> So Joseph found favor in his [Potiphar's] sight and attended him, and he made him overseer of his house and put him in charge of all that he had. From the time that he made him overseer in his house and over all that he had, the LORD blessed the Egyptian's house for Joseph's sake; the blessing of the LORD was on all that he had, in house and field. (Gen. 39:4–5 ESV)

As stewards in His house, our goal is to stand before the Lord on that great day and hear Him say, "Well done, good and faithful servant."

Flowing Out of God's Creation

Aside from the fact that all of creation testifies to the existence of a Creator, we have a biblical account in Genesis 1:1–2:4 that shows this important truth. We read that the Godhead as Trinity acted alone and of their own will—"Let Us make man in Our image, according to Our likeness" (Gen. 1:26). From the text, it is clear that there was a time when creation did not exist. Creation came about only through God's will and His spoken word. Nothing else and no one else contributed to creation: He acted alone within Himself.

The fact that there was nothing and then there was something places ownership fully in the hands of the Lord, the Creator, and nowhere else. His divine right of ownership is the very foundation of our stewardship. Where there is no divine ownership, there cannot be *true* biblical stewardship.

GOD, THE CREATOR

In a very real sense, God owns us in a way that only a Creator can—completely and rightfully. Throughout the Law and the Prophets, God repeatedly reminds us that He is the Creator, and therefore He owns us:

"The land shall not be sold in perpetuity, for the land is mine. For you are strangers and sojourners with me." (Lev. 25:23 ESV)

"Behold, to the LORD your God belong heaven and the heaven of heavens, the earth with all that is in it." (Deut. 10:14 ESV)

"It is I who by my great power and my outstretched arm have made the earth, with the men and animals that are on the earth, and I give it to whomever it seems right to me." (Jer. 27:5 ESV)[1]

Furthermore, Paul reminds us in Colossians:

> For by him all things were created, in heaven and on earth, visible and invisible, whether thrones or dominions or rulers or authorities—all things were created through him and for him. (1:16 ESV)

This complete, sovereign, authoritative ownership of God is potentially offensive to a person with a spirit of independence. But the Bible says, "Thus says God the LORD, who created the heavens . . . who gives breath to the people on it, and spirit to those who walk on it" (Isa. 42:5 ESV). God created the planet, He created the human race, and then He put breath and spirit into the people He had created. We only exist because He decided to create us in the first place.

HUMANITY'S ROLE WITHIN CREATION

Humans have a unique role within God's creation—they are part of it but also have a role of management and responsibility over it. Humanity was created lower than the angels but higher than the animal kingdom, yet we are stewards over His creation (Ps. 8:5–6). Humanity is a part of creation unlike any other, for we can choose a close personal relationship with our Creator.

It's not enough to simply understand that God has created us. We must also have a clear conviction about the dignity that God has given to us in appointing us as stewards over His creation. This is not connected to our occupation or how much education we have, but we have the greatest job of all: to enter into this dynamic of stewardship, playing a part with God in managing His creation.

God created the planet, the seas, vegetation, and animals, and then He created man and invited Adam to participate with Him in completing this creation. He gave Adam the job of naming the animals. What was the first role and responsibility Adam had in the garden of Eden? He had stewardship responsibility of the land. He had to take care of a piece of real estate called the garden of Eden, and his stewardship had responsibilities, expectations, boundaries, and guidelines. There was work to do before the fall. Adam stepped out of his job description, however, and made a decision based upon his own desire rather than God's desire. As a result, sin entered the earth. In light of God's plan, Adam's self-motivated decision was mismanagement—a failed stewardship.

We are men and women in relationship with the God of creation and with all that He created. The way we relate to all of His creation is the very foundation of stewardship. We must pay attention to this because God cares about how we relate to the environment. He cares about how we relate to our neighbor because our neighbor is part of His creation, too.

It is important that we walk in the second great commandment to love our neighbor as ourselves (Mk. 12:31), not only for love's sake, but because it is part of understanding the place we have in creation and our responsibility for it. We must keep our eyes fixed on our enthroned Creator, and with love and respect we act as proper stewards of everything within His kingdom.

Understanding our role in stewardship keeps us humble. Our relationships with friends, family, the lost, and the poor are all part of our stewardship.

God is always calling us to good stewardship, and we must respond to that call, knowing that we are only stewards because He created it all for His glory and our good. But stewardship also flows out of redemption.

Flowing Out of God's Redemption

We all have this great privilege of entering into stewardship with the Lord, using all the things He has given to us—including material possessions, such as money, houses, spiritual giftings, callings, and relationships. It is true that all of life revolves around biblical stewardship, and our reward in Christ is directly related to how we manage what we've been given regardless of the quantity.

We see that God is the Creator and owner of the earth, and we understand He has made us His managers over that creation. In the New Testament, on the other hand, we have a different reflection of God's ownership of us. We begin to see the Lord as the Redeemer of His people and the earth, and we see this issue of ownership reflected in His redemption. It is a continuation of what God began in the Old Testament, while at the same time it has several distinct features. Namely, our Creator God reveals Himself as Christ the Redeemer, where He buys back His people who have been lost to sin, which is clearly seen in the incarnation, the cross, and the bodily resurrection of Jesus Christ.

Every time I meditate on Christ's incarnation—"the Word became flesh" (Jn. 1:14)—I become overwhelmed by the thought of God becoming a man. The very fact that God became human speaks of His stewardship. Jesus, the second person of the Trinity, functioned in stewardship by knowing the will of His Father, acting upon it by becoming flesh, and dwelling among us.

In the incarnation, we see the eternal entering the temporal. We see that which is spirit entering the physical for the purpose of redeeming it. Jesus is the premier model of a servant, essentially a manager of the Father's will. He came, and He administered or obeyed His Father's will. When encouraging the Philippian believers to be like Christ Jesus, Paul spoke of Jesus' incarnation. He said:

> Let this mind be in you which was also in Christ Jesus, who, being in the form of God, did not consider it robbery to be equal with God, but made Himself of no reputation, taking the form of a bondservant, and coming in the likeness of men. And being found in appearance as a man, He humbled Himself and became obedient to the point of death, even the death of the cross. (Phil. 2:5–8)

When God comes and redeems humanity, He creates something completely new. He is not going to snatch us off a dying planet and whisk us away to an everlasting life in the clouds. He is coming once again to restore all things, and He is bringing with Him a new heaven and a new earth (Isa. 65:17; Rev. 21:1). God has always been an excellent steward of His own purposes and will continue to be.

God's taking on a body of flesh is proof that He can use the temporal and physical for the purpose of redemption. If God entered into time and space to take on flesh for the purpose of redemption, to what degree will He continue to do so in our own lives? In other words, how does God want to use our bodies, our minds, and our wills for His purposes? How does He want to use our property, automobiles, money, relationships, time, and skills to fulfill His purposes and will in the earth?

Because of the incarnation, we are now stewards with a new opportunity, in which all that we see and touch can be used for the purpose of redemption and for the fulfillment of His perfect will.

BONDSERVANTS

Paul's admonition to the Philippians was for them to have the same mind of Christ, to take the form of a bondservant. The word *servant* is the Greek word *doulos*, which actually means "slave." About ninety-nine out of a hundred Bibles will translate it as *servant*. But the word *bondservant* speaks of a voluntary slave, someone who is a slave because of love.

In the Old Testament, a servant had served his master until his time was up, and then he was able to be free. If he chose not to go free, he could go to the doorpost of the house of his master and have his master pierce his ear with an awl to become a bondservant. Out of his love, the slave was pronouncing his master's ownership over him. Once a bondservant, the slave was forever considered the owner's personal property having no rights of his own.

"Servant" in my opinion is not the best translation for our modern ears. When we hear the word *servant*, we think of service, a job, or a duty, and that would be accurate. In biblical times, when they heard the word it meant slave, owned by another, no life of one's own apart from one's master. A bondservant, however, doesn't speak of the quality of life the individual has; rather, it speaks of the master's ownership. Slaves were bought or born in their master's house. They were like purchased property.

Paul was speaking in a cultural setting in which everybody understood that slavery did not mean they were poorly treated, but that they were fully available to serve their master only. And because of this trusted relationship between the slave and the owner, the slave carried the authority of the master to buy and sell in the market under the master's name. When a slave spoke in public, representing the interests of his master, other masters responded to him as though his master were there in their midst.

Jesus did the will of His Father, and He actually expressed delight in the duty and responsibility He was given. Similarly, Paul said he was a voluntary "bondservant of Jesus Christ" (Rom. 1:1). Paul saw himself fully owned and possessed by another. This whole process does not cheapen our relationship with God or our job as His stewards; rather, our relationship with Him is full of love and honor.

Jesus did not just die in order to satisfy the wrath of God for the sins of man, although that was part of it. He was also demonstrating the love that was already in the heart of God. His stewardship of the cross was motivated by love and should inspire us to be good stewards of what He has given us, equally motivated by love. Jesus was engaged with the Father's redemptive global mission, and His stewardship of that mission led Him to a cross where tremendous love was shown. Love was making a way for us. We take our lead from Jesus and imitate Him. Therefore, let's steward well because of love, steward well because of the global mission.

Christianity is an invitation to share in the cross. We are to renounce all, take up our cross, and daily follow Him. We must live in such a way that we carry within us the death of the cross. We deny ourselves certain things, but even more so we are in a position of standing apart from ourselves and standing as wholehearted servants of God, praying, "Not our will be done, but Your will be done." Understanding this simple yet profound truth and walking in it is the very foundation of stewardship. The cross was *for* us. Jesus became a curse *for* us. His stewardship was living and dying *for* others. And our stewardship should be markedly the same.

We are bondservants of the One who bought us. If we are not our own but created by another and redeemed by another, then nothing we have in life is ours. Our time, bodies, property, gifts, relationships, jobs, callings, and any other aspect of our lives, all belong to our Lord.

When our stewardship takes on the reality of Christ's stewardship, it becomes life-changing for us. I know this to be true. I remember, on one occasion, I was approached by a person about a year after she had heard me speak on the subject of stewardship. This young woman said to me, "I wanted to let you know that your teaching on stewardship changed my life." Rarely will *a* teaching change someone's life; at best, it's impactful.

So, I replied, "Well, you mean it had an impact on you." Her response surprised me.

"No, it changed my life. Stewardship helped me realize that Jesus was my Savior but I had not made Him my Lord. I was always a giver but never talked with the Lord about managing His money.

I always spent what I wanted when I wanted; I was looking out for me. I needed to be satisfied and taken care of. When I heard the teaching on stewardship, it was like being born again. Jesus became Lord, and slowly my life began to reflect His lordship. Because my life truly belonged to the Lord, I changed how I spent my time and money. I no longer had to be constantly entertained and satisfied. First Corinthians 6:19–20 became so clear to me that I changed the way I was eating and living. As a result, I lost about eighty pounds in the coming year. It turned out that all the satisfaction, security, and identity I was looking for and reaching for in wrong ways I found in being a good steward."

THE STUFF GOD USES

God uses tangible things that we can see, touch, and smell for the purpose of global redemption. He enters into time and space, and through the frame of a human named Jesus, He brings about global redemption. Through material things like water, fish, bread, nets, homes, coins, and upper rooms, God brings about global redemption. He uses temporal items to bring about His will and His ways in the earth. This is not something God has only done sometimes, but God has always used yielded human beings to bring about His will in the earth.

Because of this, each of us can play a major role in His plan as we surrender our will to serve God's greater purpose. We can yield our pocketbook, our food, our car, our job, our time, our house, our spiritual gifts, and any other resources we have been given. When we give our time in service and our money to ministries that are proclaiming the gospel of the kingdom, we are partnering with the victory of Jesus.

Good Bible schools, missions works, and various other ministries are all playing a part in extending the victory of the cross. The kingdom of God, its message, and its victories are all advanced on the earth when we function in our roles as His stewards. If we were to fully function this way, we would be the most satisfied people on the planet, and a million other woes would also be dealt with.

Reflecting the Lordship of Christ

When we come to see Jesus as our Creator King, we understand that this world and all that is in it belongs to Him. When we are born again, there is a transfer of ownership from us to Him. If we have fully given over our lives to the King, they will be marked by our changed behavior, including but not limited to how we handle money.

John the Baptist addressed what stewardship should look like upon conversion. In his confrontation with the crowds while baptizing in the wilderness, he said:

"You brood of vipers! Who warned you to flee from the wrath to come? Bear fruits in keeping with repentance. And do not begin to say to yourselves, 'We have Abraham as our father.' For I tell you, God is able from these stones to raise up children for Abraham. Even now the axe is laid to the root of the trees. Every tree therefore that does not bear good fruit is cut down and thrown into the fire."

And the crowds asked him, "What then shall we do?" And he answered them, "Whoever has two tunics is to share with him who has none, and whoever has food is to do likewise." Tax collectors also came to be baptized and said to him, "Teacher, what shall we do?" And he said to them, "Collect no more than you are authorized to do." Soldiers also asked him, "And we, what shall we do?" And he said to them, "Do not extort money from anyone by threats or by false accusation, and be content with your wages." (Lk. 3:7–14 ESV)

People were coming out to John to be baptized, and he rebuked them, saying, "Who warned you to flee from the wrath to come?" First, John said we must bear the fruits of repentance. What are these fruits? In this passage, it is clear that sharing our food and clothing with those who have none, collecting no more taxes than what are due, taking no money for gain, and being happy with our wages are the fruit he is speaking of.

John knew that the people were not repentant because their management of money and resources had not changed. They had not transferred full ownership over to the Lord and become stewards of what was already His in the first place. What would John say to us today? Does our spending reflect the lordship of Christ?

When we see that it all belongs to the King, we will manage His money in a way that He desires. The King loves the poor, He likes honesty and contentment, and He certainly likes the good news of the kingdom.

In Luke 19:1–10, Zacchaeus was up in a tree, trying to see and hear Jesus. Jesus and the crowd came by the tree, and Jesus looked up and saw Zacchaeus. He said to him, and I am using today's vernacular here, "Zacchaeus, come down from that tree for today I am going to eat lunch with you."

At that point, the crowd started to grumble because Zacchaeus was a tax collector. When he heard their grumbling, he quickly jumped down from the tree and spoke to Jesus; his response was remarkable. He said, "Lord, Lord, I will sell all I have, give to the poor, and pay back four times what is owed."

It's important to note that Zacchaeus called Jesus *Lord*, and with this revelation, a transfer of ownership, there was a change of behavior. Jesus' response was even more remarkable "Zacchaeus today salvation has come to your home."

What was Jesus saying? Had Zacchaeus just given his way into salvation? No certainly not! Zacchaeus saw Jesus as Lord and repented.

What does the word *repent* actually mean? It means to turn, to change our mindset, to take action in another direction. When I change direction in my heart, my wallet goes along with me. We can't repent from our former lifestyles and not change the style in which we steward our money. Our spending must reflect the new lordship of Christ in our lives.

In this encounter, Jesus found the type of repentance that John was looking for in Luke 3. Zacchaeus saw who Jesus really was, and it demanded a change in his behavior. And the first change that was reflected in his life was how he was going to manage the Lord's money. Seeing the Lord caused a shift in Zacchaeus's thinking. He moved forward, determined to manage his finances according to Jesus' desire and no longer his own.

We all must "let go" of our stuff, both the rich and the poor alike. With that being said, it's still possible to be fully repentant, to fully "let go," yet be wealthy. Letting go does not necessarily equate selling everything and giving away everything we own. Letting go simply means there is a full transfer of ownership, where we become stewards, and we will faithfully obey everything Jesus asks us to do.

Jesus teaches about thirty-eight unique parables and sixteen of them deal directly with stewardship. Given the total number of Jesus' words recorded and the amount of those words spent on stewardship, we find that about 25 percent of Jesus' teaching was on stewardship. Why so much on the topic?

The answer is simple really. Arguably, Jesus' most talked about subject was the good news of the kingdom, and the Gospels make it clear that Jesus is the King over this kingdom. Stewardship is our joy-filled obedient response to our sovereign King. It is the daily demonstration of what we believe about the Lord and our relationship to Him. This is why Jesus taught about it so much.

Jesus addressed this a number of times in parables that start out with, "The kingdom of heaven is like . . ." In His parables, Jesus often used the relationship between a landowner who has gone away on a long trip and his servants to address the issue of stewardship. Take Matthew 25:14–30 for example, in the parable of the talents. He said:

> "For the kingdom of heaven is like a man traveling to a
> far country, who called his own servants and delivered
> his goods to them. And to one he gave five talents, to

another two, and to another one, to each according to his own ability; and immediately he went on a journey." (vv. 14–15)

The servant with the five talents and the servant with the two talents go and faithfully serve their absent master, producing a return on their master's investment. The servant with the one talent does nothing.

The real turning point in this story is verse 19: "After a long time the lord of those servants came and settled accounts with them." The servants with the five and the two talents, respectively, both acted with good stewardship and doubled all that they had been given. Because of their faithful service, they were given more to steward and could enter into the joy of their master.

But then the servant who had received one talent said, "'Lord, I knew you to be a hard man, reaping where you have not sown, and gathering where you have not scattered seed'" (Mt. 25:24). The one-talent servant was bound by fear. When he was confronted, he accused his master. He blamed his lord for hardness and lofty expectations. His lord, however, was anything but a tyrant; he actually liked to reward his servants. Fear is never an adequate excuse for poor stewardship.

The master then answered him. He said:

"'You wicked and lazy servant, you knew that I reap where I have not sown, and gather where I have not scattered seed. So you ought to have deposited my money with the bankers, and at my coming I would have received back my own with interest.'" (vv. 26–27)

The master ended up taking from the servant what had been given to him and gave it to the one with ten talents. In the same way, if we will not steward what the Lord has entrusted to us, He will give it to someone else. If we are not willing to seize opportunities in stewardship, then the Lord will pass them on to someone who is willing to take the risk.

Conclusion

As we have seen, we are simply stewards over God's creation. He owns all things, and He is the very One who created us, and yet He gave us a unique role to play in the earth. Though we are created like everything else we see around us, we are the pinnacle of God's creation. There is nothing else in all of creation that relates to God in the way we do—voluntarily submitting ourselves to His authority. Stewardship is simply how we live from that place of submission to God.

God's stewardship is clearly seen in the fact that Christ emptied Himself and took on the form of a slave in order to redeem humanity. We are not our own: "For you were bought at a price; therefore glorify God in your body and in your spirit, which are God's" (1 Cor. 6:20).

A steward's role was to properly manage, oversee, and govern all of his master's personal property, interests, and business affairs according to his master's will. This could have included overseeing his children, completing the bookkeeping, and paying the staff. Since God owns everything in the world, including us, we need to show love and respect by learning how to be good stewards of all that He has entrusted to us.

Jesus paid for our redemption, so our response must be to live as righteous stewards before Him. We cannot determine good stewardship based on a percentage or with a formula or by the sticker price of a particular item; we can only discover good stewardship when we walk in genuine love for our enthroned King Jesus and set out hearts on obedience. Our love-filled stewardship should shout, "Jesus is Lord!"

Stewardship, in the context of this book, matters to us because, if we are called into full-time occupational ministry, then we need to be good stewards of that calling. This would include several things but one of them for sure would be making sure the calling is properly funded.

Secondly, every born again believer has a financial stewardship in the Great Commission. So when we talk with people about giving to our ministry, we are really presenting them with a stewardship opportunity. Support raising is really two servants/stewards having a conversation to see if their stewardships overlap.

Looking Inside

- Have you given the full ownership of money, property, your body, dreams, gifting, ministry, family, and time over to the Lord? (see Lk. 14:26–33)

- What areas of your life are not yet submitted to the lordship of Christ?

- What could you do to improve your stewardship?

- If you are called to full-time ministry, are you properly stewarding that assignment by being properly trained, equipped, and funded? How could you improve?

Taking Action

Spend fifteen minutes a day looking at one of the following passages of Scripture: Matthew 25:14–30; Matthew 25:31–46; Luke 10:25–37; Luke 16:19–31. Read through each passage a couple of times, and then ask the following questions and write down your answers.

- What is the context of the parable, or what question prompted Jesus to teach the parable?

- Who are the main characters in the parable?

- What comparisons are being made, or what ones do you see, between the characters?

- Do you see any patterns in these parables?

- What is the outcome of those who do not steward?

CHAPTER FOUR

Old Testament Pictures of Partnership

God wants our agreement. The highest agreement a follower of Christ can give is martyrdom. The second highest is a financial commitment.

When we go to the Scriptures, we discover God has a way of moving His mission forward. In fact, a pattern emerges as we study the Word. Throughout the pages of the Old Testament, our focus for this chapter, we are given pictures of partnership as we view the story of God's relationship with the children of Israel and see how various leaders raised the funds needed to fulfill God-given directives. These pictures outline the pattern that will serve as the model for the first full-time occupational ministers, namely those in the Levitical priesthood. Its very existence in Scripture gave New Testament workers (and gives us today) a confidence that team ministry was (and is) an age-old pattern established by God.

What is the pattern that emerges?

The biblical pattern we see in the Old Testament has four specific points:

1. God gives a vision to a person.
2. The person gathers people together to share the vision.

3. God stirs the hearts of the people.

4. The people give as they are invited by that person to partner in the vision.

As we will soon see, this pattern is apparent in the way Moses, Aaron, the Levitical priesthood, David, and Nehemiah—among others—were enabled to fulfill their assignments.

The Tabernacle and Its Workers

Shortly after Israel came out of Egyptian bondage, the Lord spoke to Moses, telling him to build a tabernacle where He could dwell among the people of Israel. God revealed the heavenly temple to Moses and instructed him to build the earthly tabernacle according to its pattern. In Exodus 25, we see how God spoke to Moses and instructed him, in turn, to speak to Israel, telling them all that God had spoken and that they were to bring Him an offering.

Offerings had been given in the past, but this was the first time we read where God had commanded that an offering be taken. There was a specific purpose for the offering. It was to be collected for the construction of the tabernacle and the establishment of the priesthood. We read, "Then the LORD spoke to Moses, saying 'Speak to the children of Israel, that they bring Me an offering. From everyone who gives it *willingly* with his heart you shall take My offering'" (Ex. 25:1–2).

Later, in Exodus 35, Moses spoke to the congregation of the children of Israel, saying,

> "This is the thing which the LORD commanded, saying: 'Take from among you an offering to the LORD. Whoever is of a willing heart, let him bring it as an offering to the LORD: gold, silver, and bronze . . .'" (vv. 4–5)

And after Moses gave further instructions, we are told:

> Then everyone came whose heart was *stirred*, and everyone whose spirit was *willing*, and they brought the LORD's offering for the work of the tabernacle of meeting, for all its service, and for the holy garments. They came, both men and women, as many as had a **willing** heart . . . (Ex. 35:21–22)

Moses shared the vision God had given him, and the people responded accordingly. It is interesting to note that God didn't just put it into the hearts of the people to give to the work of building the tabernacle, though He could have done that. Instead, He chose to have Moses convey the vision first. Then He prompted or stirred the people to respond in giving their offerings. It was Moses who first shared what God had spoken to him, and God stirred the hearts of the people to respond in giving. Without the sharing of the vision, there would have been no stirring of the people's hearts.

We must notice, however, that there were some people whose hearts were not stirred to contribute. How do we make this deduction? We are told that "as many as had a *willing* heart" gave to the work, which suggests that there were those whose hearts were not willing; in other words, they were not disposed to give to the work of the Lord.

When we share the vision God has given us, not everyone will be stirred or willing to give. This was the case as I built my own partnership team. Most of the individuals I was absolutely convinced would partner with me—because of our friendship, my past ministry, or my personal impact on their family—did not partner with me, but thankfully some did. We shouldn't take personally someone's not partnering with us, because not everyone will respond the way we might expect. It is our job to share what God has put into our hearts, and it is God's job to stir. We need to leave it up to Him, for He knows how to do it best.

I have seen this stirring of the Lord happen in meetings when vision is clearly presented. People, who prior to the meeting made it clear they were unable to give, listened to stories of what the Lord was doing and what the missionary speaker was called to do when, suddenly, they became stirred and gave financial gifts or became partners. I have even witnessed face-to-face vision sharing where the ones receiving the information looked bored and disinterested only to transition into readiness to partner. So God can ignite hearts to participate with us in our mission as we are faithful to share it.

Not only did God provide for the building of the tabernacle, but He also arranged for the provision of those who would serve full-time in the tabernacle. God created a financial system through the giving of the people that would sustain the priesthood for generations to come. Speaking specifically to Aaron in the presence of his brother, Moses, the Lord said:

> "Behold, I have given the children of Levi all the tithes in Israel as an inheritance in return for the work which they perform, the work of the tabernacle of meeting. Hereafter

the children of Israel shall not come near the tabernacle of meeting, lest they bear sin and die. But the Levites shall perform the work of the tabernacle of meeting, and they shall bear their iniquity; it shall be a statute forever, throughout your generations, that among the children of Israel they shall have no inheritance. For the tithes of the children of Israel, which they offer up as a heave offering to the Lord, I have given to the Levites as an inheritance; therefore I have said to them, 'Among the children of Israel they shall have no inheritance.'" (Num. 18:21–24)

We can also see from the passage in Numbers 18 that it was the Lord who gave all the tithes in Israel to the Levites in exchange for the work they performed. Not only that, but He gave it to them as an inheritance. Like any inheritance, the priesthood would be passed down from generation to generation. The Levites did not receive land as the other tribes did, land that could be farmed and developed so they could earn a living from it, but rather they received a perpetual priesthood. The priesthood was their full-time occupation and source of provision, and was what the Lord had called them to.

God wanted this priesthood before Him perpetually. How did that happen? After all, a man had to take care of himself and his family, and if he didn't have ground that he could work or develop, what did he do? God in His desire to have this priesthood before Him continually, ministering to Him night and day, provided a way for the priest to do it—through the tithes of the people of Israel.

The tithes were given to God as an offering, and then it was God who shared this offering with the priest. This is an important point, especially when we are talking about funding any worker in the kingdom of God. When we give from a willing heart, we are giving to God. That means we are not giving to people, and we are not giving to ideas, personal plans, or agendas. We are not giving with conditions so that our interests or desires are met. When we give, we are giving to God, and God chooses to share our giving with His workers. If we are looking to go forward in missions, we must recognize that, when people give, they are not giving to us; they are giving their gifts to God. Understanding this should be both liberating and humbling to us.

We can see from the passage in Numbers 18 that the tithes had always been a means of support for the Levites who worked in the tabernacle of meeting. It was their means of provision for themselves and for all that was needed to do their job. So the tithe system was created in order to sustain the first full-time occupational workers in the Bible. By funding the priesthood, God was creating and sustaining it in perpetuity.

The reason that is important for us is this: God calls people into occupational ministry. He has a plan for them and a way for them to be funded so they can serve Him full-time. It is not a mystery; in fact, the pattern God established is clear. The responsibility does not lie completely on the worker but upon every member of the Body of Christ. We all must obey and do our part to see the end-time harvest come in. God wants to build His kingdom with the voluntary agreement of His people.

David's Heart to Build a House

Another place where we see God providing for His workers is in David's desire to build a temple, a dwelling place for God. David had it in his heart to build God a house where He could dwell among His people forever. He was uncomfortable with his own living in a house lined with cedar panels while God was dwelling in curtains (see 2 Sam. 7:2). But David was not the one who was going to build the temple, for God planned that his son, Solomon, would build it. At the dedication of the temple, Solomon said:

> "Now it was in the heart of my father David to build a temple for the name of the LORD God of Israel. But the LORD said to my father David, 'Whereas it was in your heart to build a temple for My name, you did well that it was in your heart. Nevertheless you shall not build the temple, but your son who will come from your body, he shall build the temple for My name.'" (1 Kgs. 8:17–19)

The reason David was not the one to build the temple was because of his involvement in war, in shedding the blood of others. During a time of peace, his son would build the temple for God's name (see 1 Chr. 22:7–11).

Even though David would not be the one to build the temple, he was allowed to prepare for the project. In First Chronicles 22–27, David made plans with stonecutters, craftsmen, and all types of skilled workmen. He also organized the Levites, priests, and musicians. After all the preparations were made, David gathered together the leaders of Israel to share what was on his heart (see 1 Chr. 28:1).

David didn't gather together all the men of Israel; instead, he gathered together the leaders of Israel. These were men with whom David had a long history. He trusted them to serve Solomon in the same way they had faithfully served him throughout his reign. Once gathered together, David shared his heart and told the story of how God appointed Solomon as builder and king (see 1 Chr. 28:2–10). In front of all the leaders, David shared all the plans, blueprints, and materials with Solomon (see 1 Chr. 28:11–19). He then encouraged his son and gave him the divisions of priests and Levites, gave him all the "willing" craftsmen, and gave him the materials (see 1 Chr. 28:21–22).

David went on to list all the financial resources of his own private treasury that he proffered to the project, and then he clearly invited those assembled together to give (see 1 Chr. 29:1–5). David shared what he had in his heart to do, thereby inviting others to be a part of that vision by their willingly giving to the work of God. We read:

> Then the leaders of the fathers' houses, leaders of the tribes of Israel, the captains of thousands and of hundreds, with the officers over the king's work, offered willingly. They gave for the work of the house of God five thousand talents and ten thousand darics of gold, ten thousand talents of silver, eighteen thousand talents of bronze, and one hundred thousand talents of iron. And whoever had *precious* stones gave *them* to the treasury of the house of the Lord, into the hand of Jehiel the Gershonite. Then *the people rejoiced, for they had offered willingly*, because with a loyal heart they had *offered willingly* to the Lord; and King David also rejoiced greatly. (1 Chr. 29:6–9)

Because the vision was laid out clearly, the men caught the vision, rejoiced, and then gave extravagantly. The amount of gold that David supplied was three thousand talents, and the leadership tendered another five thousand talents. One talent of gold was equal to five thousand days wages, which means that the total amount given by David and the leaders was forty million days wages. Were this offering to be taken today, at an average wage of two hundred dollars a day, it would equal to about eight billion dollars. And that's only counting the gold and no other precious metals or stones that were given.

In a similar way, although on a much smaller scale, I have seen the people of God respond with extravagance to the opportunity to join God in what He is doing. It was 2008, and some friends of mine had been drawn into an incredible situation in Asia. They were given tremendous favor and were making a real impact in a region that had been closed to the gospel.

From the United States, we watched the situation unfold over the course of months, and with each passing week the move of God grew stronger and stronger. As this story in Asia was emerging, so was the opportunity for the Church to be involved. During that time, I shared testimonies with a pastor friend about the move of God in Asia, so he invited me to come and share with his church. I shared how God was doing awesome things with this little Asian church of about seventy people. As I spoke, the Holy Spirit stirred the congregation. I invited them to be a part of what was happening and asked them to give toward the work in Asia. That morning, the congregation gave an offering of twenty-six thousand dollars!

The Asian church storyline continued to unfold. The Lord opened doors there that no man could shut. I continued to share with my friend, and he invited me back to his church the following month to share updates about the rapidly growing story. On this second visit, his little church gave twenty-eight thousand dollars. As with the previous month, this gift was an offering above and beyond the normal Sunday morning offering.

By that time, the incredible story was several months along, the testimonies were amazing, and the move of God was clear and powerful. My friends in Asia had gained the confidence and trust of government leaders. It was at this point that this country, which had been closed to the gospel, asked my friends to bring a team and share the gospel with their nation.

I shared the news with my pastor friend, and he invited me yet a third time in three months to share this story of God's goodness with his church. I went this third time and shared the incredible open door for the gospel that had come through the faithful service of my friends. I invited this church to respond to the open door and help send this missional team to a previously closed off country. The church responded with a gift of forty-six thousand dollars this time.

This one little church had given one hundred thousand dollars in just ninety days! I realize that one hundred thousand dollars can be the weekly offering of some megachurches, but for this blue-collar church it was a great response of worship and agreement. Just like the labor of my friends, I too believe that this offering to the Lord was a sweet smelling aroma.

Likewise, David rejoiced not just over what the people gave, but over their willingness to give. After the offering, he turned to the Lord and said, "Both riches and honor come from You, and You reign over all. In Your hand is power and might; in Your hand it is to make great and to give strength to all" (1 Chr. 29:12). And then he said, "But who am I, and who are my people, that we should be able to offer so willingly as this? *For all things come from You*, and of Your own we have given You" (v. 14).

Oh, there is a pattern emerging here, isn't there? God gives vision to a person, and when that vision is shared, the Lord stirs the people's hearts. And those whose hearts are stirred, offer willingly to the work that God wants to do in their midst. Seeing the vision of the Lord or hearing about it being realized provokes a desire within us to give unto the work of the Lord, which makes making financial commitments to the work of the Lord exciting, joyful, and biblically normal.

Cyrus and the Building of the Second Temple

After the children of Israel were in captivity, part of the rebuilding process of the temple happened in much the same way. We can see this in Ezra, where the Lord uses Cyrus the king to accomplish His purpose and will in the earth (see Ezra 1:1–11).

King Cyrus came to understand that he would play a role in the rebuilding of the kingdom. The Lord spoke to and moved upon a nonbelieving king to fulfill prophecy. In Ezra 1:2–4, we read the following proclamation:

Thus says Cyrus king of Persia: The LORD, the God of heaven, has given me all the kingdoms of the earth, and he has charged me to build him a house at Jerusalem, which is in Judah. Whoever is among you of all his people, may his God be with him, and let him go up to Jerusalem, which is in Judah, and rebuild the house of the LORD, the God of Israel—he is the God who is in Jerusalem. *And let each survivor, in whatever place he sojourns, be assisted by the men of his place with silver and gold, with goods and with beasts, besides freewill offerings for the house of God that is in Jerusalem.* (ESV)

Cyrus spoke to the Israelites who were in captivity, telling them to decide among themselves who was going to journey to Israel and rebuild the temple and who was going to stay behind. Those people who chose to go were to be "assisted by the men of this place with silver and gold, with goods and beasts."

Furthermore, their support was to be in addition to the "freewill offerings." This would mean that, in restoring the temple, there would also be a restoration of the priesthood as well as the tithe system with freewill offerings. The support Cyrus was requiring was in addition to, and not a replacement of, the tithes and offerings that were already being given.

The story goes on:

Then rose up the heads of the fathers' houses of Judah and Benjamin, and the priests and the Levites, everyone whose spirit *God had stirred* to go up to rebuild the house of the LORD that is in Jerusalem. *And all who were about them aided them* with vessels of silver, with gold, with goods, with beasts, and with costly wares, *besides all that was freely offered.* (Ezra 1:5–6 ESV)

We can see that it was God who was doing all the "stirring": first with Cyrus for building the temple and making declarations, and then with Israel and some of the people to go rebuild the temple.

As if that were not enough, Cyrus, cooperating with the building of the temple, returned all the articles and vessels that Nebuchadnezzar had carried away from Jerusalem, which were needed for restoring all the sacrificial offerings in the temple:

> Cyrus the king also brought out the vessels of the house of the LORD that Nebuchadnezzar had carried away from Jerusalem and placed in the house of his gods. Cyrus king of Persia brought these out in the charge of Mithredath the treasurer, who counted them out to Sheshbazzar the prince of Judah. And this was the number of them: 30 basins of gold, 1,000 basins of silver, 29 censers, 30 bowls of gold, 410 bowls of silver, and 1,000 other vessels; all the vessels of gold and of silver were 5,400. All these did Sheshbazzar bring up, when the exiles were brought up from Babylonia to Jerusalem. (vv. 7–11 ESV)

So we can see from Israel's return from captivity and their rebuilding of the temple, God not only stirred the hearts of His people to give and to go, but He also used a nonbelieving king to provide for the rebuilding of His temple. Once the vision was shared, God stirred the hearts of people to provide and, thus, move the vision forward.

Nehemiah's Desire to Rebuild Jerusalem

Nehemiah was another man who heard from God, got a vision from God, and then shared that vision with the people. Nehemiah heard about the ruins of destruction in Jerusalem; then, he became depressed:

> Therefore the king said to me, "Why is your face sad, since you are not sick? This is nothing but sorrow of heart." So I became dreadfully afraid, and said to the king, "May the king live forever! Why should my face not be sad, when the city, the place of my fathers' tombs, lies waste, and its gates are burned with fire?" Then the king said to me, "What do you request?" So I prayed to the God of heaven. And I said to the king, "If it pleases the king, and if your servant has found favor in your sight, I ask that you send me to Judah, to the city of my fathers' tombs, that I may rebuild it." Then the king said to me (the queen also sitting beside him), "How long will your journey be? And when will you return?" So it pleased the king to send me; and I set him a time. (Neh. 2:2–6)

Nehemiah responded to his captor king's inquiry about Jerusalem, asking the king for protection so that he could accomplish the work of rebuilding Jerusalem, the wall, and the temple. Then Nehemiah asked for further help from the king:

> Furthermore I said to the king, "If it pleases the king, let letters be given to me for the governors of the region beyond the River, that they must permit me to pass through till I come to Judah, and a letter to Asaph the keeper of the king's forest, that he must give me timber to make beams for the gates of the citadel which pertains to the temple, for the city wall, and for the house that I will occupy." And the king granted them to me according to the good hand of my God upon me. Then I went to the governors in the region beyond the River, and gave them the king's letters. Now the king had sent captains

of the army and horsemen with me. When Sanballat the Horonite and Tobiah the Ammonite official heard of it, they were deeply disturbed that a man had come to seek the well-being of the children of Israel. (vv. 7–10)

After Nehemiah cast the vision about the temple and its restoration, he invited the people to participate in giving toward that vision. Even under intense pressure, they ended up building the wall with a trowel in one hand and a sword in the other. When they were done rebuilding the wall, Nehemiah next set his focus on the temple and all they had to rebuild there. He cast vision again, and then asked for Israel's involvement.

When all the work was done, Nehemiah returned to his captor king again for some time. But when he came back to Israel after several years, he encountered some priests who were working in the field. He asked the priests why they were in the fields working and not working in the temple (see Neh. 13:6–12). The priests basically had one response: the people had stopped tithing.

In Nehemiah's absence, the people of Israel had lost vision, and when they lost vision, they lost their commitment to give. Nehemiah didn't rebuke the priests for a lack of faith; rather, he told them to return to the temple, and he would take care of the tithe. We can see here that there is a correlation among vision, agreement, the restraint of commitment, and the work moving forward.

Other Offerings for God's Servants

Even beyond the tithe that went to sustain the priesthood, we also see gifts/provision being given to support God's servants in the Old Testament. I am thinking specifically of the prophets. We find an example of an offering or gift given to a prophet in First Samuel, where Saul and his servant were sent out to find his father's donkeys that had wandered off. After searching for some time without success, they decided to go to a nearby city where they knew a man of God was living.

But they had a dilemma. Apparently, Saul thought they needed to have some sort of gift to give this "man of God" or prophet. So he said, "But look, if we go, what shall we bring the man? For the bread in our vessels is all gone, and there is no present to bring to the man of God. What do we have?" (1 Sam. 9:7).

The servant offered a solution to their dilemma. He said, "Look, I have here at hand one-fourth of a shekel of silver. I will give that to the man of God, to tell us our way" (v. 8).

Saul and his servant didn't want to go to the prophet unless they had a gift to share. But where did this idea of providing a gift or money to a prophet come from? There is no indication from the Law that a prophet was to be provided for, and there was no instruction on how he was to be supported. But something had come into the Hebrew culture that made it conditional for individuals to go to the prophet only if they brought some sort of gift.

In a later Old Testament story, we read about the woman in Shunem who convinced her husband to add a room onto their house for the prophet Elisha to stay when he was in town (see 2 Kgs. 4:8–11). Building a room on a house in that day would have been a great expense. It was no small act, costing this woman and her husband something. The act, in and of itself, demonstrated that the woman and her husband valued the prophet and his gifting. They wanted to see his ministry move forward. Their financial commitment was an agreement with God and His worker.

So there were prophets in the Old Testament, in addition to the priesthood, that were supported by God's people. How this idea of offering finances or accommodations to a person sent by God came to be is uncertain. Is it possible this understanding of supporting or gifting ministers and their ministries came through the practiced tithing pattern for the priesthood? I think so. I believe it was worked into the Hebrew culture even though it was not required in the Law. When the people saw an individual as sent by God, they saw the value of the person or gift sent to them. They became aware of the calling, gifting, and purpose of the servant of God. I believe God then stirred their hearts to make some type of contribution or provision. And they did so when given the opportunity.

Conclusion

Obeying the Lord and working with Him to fulfill His will for global restoration requires teamwork—the family of God working together. God wants to build, but He wants to build with the voluntary agreement of His people.

The first offering that God commanded to be taken was for the building of the tabernacle and for the sustaining of the priesthood. It was a voluntary offering, where people who were willing to give gave. And they gave when their hearts were stirred after they heard the presentation of the vision.

When we share God's vision, then He stirs hearts. The biblical four-point model of partnership includes God's giving a vision to His servant, His servant gathering people together and sharing the vision with them, God stirring their hearts to give, and then His servant inviting others to be a part of the vision through their contributions.

Looking Inside

- Moses, David, and Nehemiah were men with vision. What's your vision?

- David prepared with all his might. What must you do to prepare with all your might?

- How do you feel about making a clear and direct invitation, asking people to give toward what God has called you to do?

- What financial commitments are you making?

- Have you heard missionary stories that stirred you and, as a result, you gave financially? Why wouldn't others be stirred in a similar way by your missionary story and give?

Taking Action

1. Take your answers to the questions above and turn them into prayer.

2. Spend fifteen minutes a day for the next three weeks, asking God for clarity of vision and confessing any fears of rejection you might feel. Trust Him to heal that area of your heart.

3. Ask the Lord for grace to make financial commitments in the Great Commission or toward the poor, and ask the Lord for faith concerning His provision for you as a worker.

CHAPTER FIVE

Teamwork in the New Testament

If you want to go fast, go alone; if you want to go far, go together.
–African proverb

Make no mistake, there is a significant culture of partnership found in the pages of the New Testament. We can clearly see the Old Testament pattern of God's sustaining workers in the priesthood carry on through the lives of Christ, the disciples, and the believers of the early church. I want us to look at the scriptural culture of the New Testament, discussing the numerous instances of partnership and its spiritual fruit as seen in the lives of Jesus, the apostle Paul, and the apostle John.

Jesus' Partnership Team

When we read Luke 8, we find Jesus and His disciples traveling from city to city, and they were not traveling alone. We are presented with a group of fellow travelers who, in fact, provided for the needs of Jesus and His disciples:

Soon afterward [Jesus] went on through cities and villages, proclaiming and bringing the good news of the kingdom of God. And the twelve were with him, and also some women who had been healed of evil spirits and infirmities: Mary, called Magdalene, from whom seven demons had gone out, and Joanna, the wife of Chuza, Herod's household manager, and Susanna, and many others, *who provided for them out of their means.* (vv. 1–3 ESV)

Jesus actually did not sustain Himself, or the lives of His disciples, by way of miracles. Although they did miracles from time to time, there are only about five miracles where Jesus and His disciples actually benefited from the miracle itself, such as in the multiplication of bread. But that wasn't the point of the miracle, nor was it the provision model for Jesus or His disciples.

We see from this passage in Luke that there was a group of people Jesus knew by name—most of them women—who, from their means, provided for Him and His disciples. This means that Jesus—God in the flesh—put Himself in a position of being dependent on other people to sustain His life and ministry. God the Father was providing for God the Son through the giving of the saints. It was neither cutting edge nor strange at the time, as we have seen this pattern well established throughout the Old Testament. He was not introducing a new model here. But why was Jesus being provided for in this way? He could have easily supported Himself through His carpenter job as a self-funded minister, but He didn't. Once He left secular work, Jesus never returned to it again.

Sometimes, when people have worked in the marketplace for a number of years and the Lord calls them into full-time occupational ministry, they can be fearful as to whether or not the Lord is actually going to provide for them. They may struggle with feelings of guilt due to their not making their own living to support their fulfilling God's call. They may even feel as if they are acting like or being seen by others as a charity case. This is all wrong thinking. I learned this lesson in a dynamic way.

I had worked in the aerospace industry for seventeen years when the Lord called me to ministry. I was moving into a missions context, where I needed to raise my own financial support. On my very first partnership meeting, I visited the home of some dear friends. Within two minutes of my being in the door, they handed me a check for two hundred and fifty dollars and said, "We believe in you and what you're doing. We're going to send two hundred and fifty dollars every month." I was shocked. I looked at my friend and his wife and their small children, and all I could think of was the sacrifice they were making for me. They were doing without something so that I could have provision. This thought caused me to start weeping, which got so bad that it made my friends uncomfortable. They mercifully asked if I would like to finish the meeting some other time. With tears, I nodded silently and began my way home.

I would like to say I stopped crying once I got in my car, but the fact is I cried all the way home, humbled by the thought that someone would even give to me. I also couldn't shake the thought that someone was doing without because of their providing for me.

I went to bed that night, and when I awoke the next morning, I saw the check on the kitchen counter and began to weep again. This time I cried all the way out the door and on into my drive to work. I really tried to stop crying, believe me, but I was unsuccessful, at least until just before arriving at work.

Upon entering my workplace, I immediately encountered my supervisor. As he was talking to me, I could feel the weeping coming on again. I couldn't suppress it any longer, and my cry burst out suddenly, and with volume! I turned and walked away from my supervisor while he was in midsentence, and as I did I felt everyone staring at me. I hurried to the men's room, went inside, gained control of myself, and headed back out to the shop floor. Then I began to feel the weeping coming on again, and suddenly I heard the Lord speak to me. With a displeased tone, He said, "Hey, stop your crying!"

Shocked, I said "Lord?"

"Stop your crying," His reply was firm. It was at that moment that I knew I was about to learn a lesson but had no idea what the lesson was, which made me very nervous.

Cautiously, I asked, "Lord, what are You saying?"

The Lord continued to speak in my spirit, asking me a series of questions: "Do you remember that you have no education yet have one of the best jobs in the city?"

"Yes, Lord," I replied.

"That was Me," He said. "Do you realize that you have never missed work due to injury or prolonged illness—that was Me. You've never had to cross a picket line; you've never been laid off or had to draw unemployment—that was Me." Then He said, "I have been giving you checks for seventeen years, and not once did you weep over them. Why are you weeping now?"

Understanding hit me immediately and painfully. The reason for the Lord's kind and gentle rebuke was that I was operating under the delusion that, while in the marketplace, I was providing for myself. Once I moved into ministerial service, people were providing for me. Both of these thoughts were wrong. The Lord had been and always will be my Provider, regardless of my occupation. My tears were not of gratitude to the Lord, but rather from my flesh being humbled by the charity of people. That was a wrong perspective, and the Lord was rebuking me for it.

On that day, it all changed for me. I understood God had already been a faithful Provider for years; there was no reason to believe He wouldn't continue to be. Additionally, my ministry work was real work, worthy of a wage that God was going to give me through the giving of His saints. From that day forward, I never again had feelings of embarrassment, shame, or anything like that. Instead, I became a grateful worker who was called of God and sustained by Him.

Why did Jesus continue to move forward in ministry without working a secular job and funding Himself? Though the answer could be varied, part of it is found in the fact that supporting workers was nearly a two-thousand-year-old ministry at that point. And ministry has never been about the individual, but about the Body of Christ as a whole, the family of God coming into agreement with the vision God gives. We all have a need to give, and we all have a need to receive. The Lord has fashioned His Body to be interdependent with each another. And Jesus showed us this in the way He allowed people to sow into His life and help support Him while He gave all of His time and attention to His Father's mission. He also demonstrated this by passing the same model on to His disciples.

Sending the Disciples

About fourteen to eighteen months into Jesus' ministry, He sent out His disciples on a ministry assignment. He had been communicating the gospel, moving in power, raising the dead, and healing the sick. It was time for His disciples do the same. So we read in Matthew 10 that Jesus sent out the Twelve with these instructions:

> "Do not go to Gentile regions and do not enter any Samaritan town. Go instead to the lost sheep of the house of Israel. As you go, preach this message: 'The kingdom of heaven is near!' Heal the sick, raise the dead, cleanse lepers, cast out demons. Freely you received, freely give. Do not take gold, silver, or copper in your belts, no bag for the journey, or an extra tunic, or sandals or staff, *for the worker deserves his provisions.* Whenever you enter a town or village, find out who is worthy there and stay with them until you leave." (vv. 5–11 NET)

Here was the disciples' first ministry assignment, so Jesus gave a clear command to them. We tend to focus on the first part of these verses and say, "Jesus commanded us to heal the sick, preach the kingdom of heaven, and deliver those who are demonized." But just as verses five through eight are commands from Jesus, so is the latter part of this passage (vv. 9–11).

When it comes to the role of funding in missions, the Matthew 10 passage of Scripture is often taught as Jesus' sending out missionaries who are to live by faith alone. Essentially, this suggests those sent are to just go preach and not worry about money because God will take care of their needs. But that is not what Jesus was saying in the passage. His wasn't a command to "purseless or shoeless missions." Rather, as we will discuss more fully in chapter 7, Jesus was telling them to leave their *own* resources at home *because* a worker is worthy of his wage.

Why weren't the disciples to take anything with them when they went out on their assignment? The key to understanding this passage is in verse ten and is contained in the word *for*. The reason Jesus didn't want the disciples taking their own money was because they deserved their pay. Part of their assignment was securing provision for themselves along the way. In the same way that they were commanded to preach, heal the sick, and cast out demons, they were also commanded to find out who was worthy and stay with them in that city (v. 11).

Why didn't Jesus tell them to take what they already had and work along the way? If they had done so, they would have been stepping away from the need for agreement and the need to depend upon others. Jesus was saying to them, "I don't want you self-funding your assignment. You're working, and a worker deserves his pay." The reason for not taking money wasn't primarily about building "super faith" in their hearts, although I'm sure their faith was built by the provision. The reason for their not taking money was about their being worthy of receiving pay for the work they were doing, namely, preaching the gospel, healing the sick, raising the dead, and casting out demons. Additionally, it was important that those who had ears to hear responded in agreement with some measure of support.

Jesus told them they were to find out who was worthy in every town they entered, and then stay with those individuals while in that town. The question naturally arises here, how did they find out who was worthy in each town they entered? They would need to talk to people. At some point, they would have to either engage people in their homes or in the marketplace, and they would have to introduce themselves and talk about the fact that Jesus had sent them on this assignment. During some point in the conversation, they would have to describe their call from God, what He had sent them to do, and share the vision He had put in their heart. Even if they didn't initiate one-on-one dialogue, their work for the Lord could have been noised around the town, stirring the hearts of some to approach them, but there still of necessity would have been some kind of sharing of vision and mission.

The disciples had been given an assignment from God, and they wanted to obey what Jesus commanded them. In love-filled obedience, they went forward and found people with whom they would share their assignment, inviting them to believe and be part of the mission of God. The provision was already there before they ever left on their assignment. God always provides for the commission. If we are called and serving the Lord, the provision is already there; we just do our part and find out who is worthy. Finding the provision that is already there is part of the assignment; it's lifting the lid, if we will recall from the introduction.

Jesus was not announcing the no purse, no shoes, and no money model of ministry. Practical items like proper gear, tools, money, and so forth are good, and they are needed for ministry. In fact, Jesus Himself was properly equipped and funded as He engaged in the work that Father had sent Him to do. Remember His fellow travelers in Luke 8? They made provision for Him. Jesus had shoes and a moneybag, of which Judas was the treasurer. Why would He have a treasurer? It was not because He was broke and didn't have need for money. A person has a treasurer because he or she has money coming in *and* going out.

Paul's Partnership with Various Churches

This model of ministry wasn't the pattern just for Jesus and His disciples, but others throughout the New Testament followed the same pattern. For example, Paul had been ministering in a particular region for some time, and his ministry there was drawing to a close. His plan was to go on to Spain, but on the way he wanted to stop by Rome and visit the church there. Before he left for Spain, he wrote to the Romans, revealing something important about resourcing the worker. He penned:

> For this reason I also have been much hindered from coming to you. But now no longer having a place in these parts, and having a great desire these many years to come to you, whenever I journey to Spain, I shall come to you. For I hope to see you on my journey, and *to be helped on my way there by you*, if first I may enjoy your company for a while. (Rom. 15:22–24)

HIS ASSISTANCE FROM THE CHURCH AT ROME

Paul had something specific in mind when he wrote "and to be helped on my way there by you." This could have included finances, shelter, housing, transportation, clothing—and any other practical needs that may have arisen along the way. We don't really know all that was summed up in that phrase, but we do know he was hoping they would help him on his way to Spain. Even though the church in Rome was a group of people Paul had never visited, met, or ministered to before, he was still asking them for assistance.

The Greek phrase, *and to be helped on my way*, is the word *propempō*, which is translated into several words in English, such as brought, being brought, bring forth, sent forth, accompanied, and supported. This phrase, then, could include prayer support, moral support or encouragement, monetary support, or also accompaniment along the journey. Paul was asking people whom he had never met to support him in various ways as he traveled through on his way to Spain.

PAUL'S RELATIONSHIP TO THE PHILIPPIANS

Philippians 4 is probably the clearest, most descriptive account of the working relationship between a missionary and his partnership team contained in the New Testament. Paul wrote:

> I have great joy in the Lord because now at last you have again expressed your concern for me. (Now I know you were concerned before but had no opportunity to do anything.) (v. 10 NET)

Paul had great joy, why? Because the saints had again shown their love for him by sending a financial gift to him. He went on further to clarify his point:

> I am not saying this because I am in need, for I have learned to be content in any circumstance. I have experienced times of need and times of abundance. In any and every circumstance I have learned the secret of contentment, whether I go satisfied or hungry, have plenty or nothing. I am able to do all things through the one who strengthens me. Nevertheless, you did well to share with me in my trouble. (vv. 11–14 NET)

Paul said their giving was a job well done (v. 14). He was not telling them this because he was in some kind of need; in fact, he was doing okay at the moment. Sure, Paul had his ups and downs in ministry—he had experienced lack in his life—but he had learned how to be content. He didn't say it *wasn't necessary* for them to share in his trouble; but he said they *had done well to share* in his trouble. And then he further commended them with this:

> And as you Philippians know, at the beginning of my gospel ministry, when I left Macedonia, *no church shared with me in this matter of giving and receiving except you alone.* (v. 15 NET)

Paul then referred to the partnership he had shared with the Philippians over the years. At this point in his life, he had been in apostolic ministry for about twenty-five years, and since its inception the church at Philippi had been in partnership with him: "from the beginning no church shared with me in this matter of giving and receiving except you alone."

The Greek word Paul used in the phrase, no *church* had shared with me, is *koinōneō*. It means to share, distribute, do together with, and participate in. This word speaks of co-laboring, working together, teamwork, and partnership.[1] More than that, *koinōneō* means that we have linked arms together and have put our hands to the plow. Paul understood that he was an apostle plowing ground, but he used this word to let them know he didn't plow alone. The Philippians had plowed with him.

Paul alluded in our text to another time when he was serving in Thessalonica—one of the places where he made tents. He acknowledged he was supported once again by the Philippians. Anytime they shared a gift with Paul, it contributed something to their spiritual account:

> For even in Thessalonica on more than one occasion you sent something for my need. I do not say this because I am seeking a gift. Rather, I seek the credit that abounds to your account. (vv. 16–17 NET)

When we support the work of the gospel, God sees it, notes it, and will later reward us for our giving. These people who were financial partners with Paul were coworkers together with him; therefore, they would be rewarded for their labor, just as Paul was going to be rewarded for his:

> For I have received everything, and I have plenty. I have all I need because I received from Epaphroditus what you sent—a fragrant offering, an acceptable sacrifice, very pleasing to God. And my God will supply your every need according to his glorious riches in Christ Jesus. May glory be given to God our Father forever and ever. Amen. (vv. 18–20 NET)

Paul then assured the Philippians that he had everything he needed *because* of the gift they had sent with Epaphroditus. Paul described the gift as a fragrant offering and an acceptable sacrifice, which was well pleasing to God. Because of the gift, Paul lacked nothing; he had everything he needed. So we can see that supporting a worker is actually a gift to God, and it is well pleasing to Him.

PAUL'S LETTERS TO TIMOTHY AND TITUS

Paul also addressed the same issue in his first letter to Timothy:

> Elders who provide effective leadership must be counted worthy of double honor, *especially those who work hard in speaking and teaching*. For the scripture says, "Do not muzzle an ox while it is treading out the grain," and, "The worker deserves his pay." (1 Tim. 5:17–18 NET)

Elders who provided effective leadership were counted worthy of double honor. The phrase, *especially those who work hard in speaking and teaching*, may be pointing to the existence of some elders whose teaching and speaking was less visible and their role more supportive in nature. In Church culture today, we are used to giving the most honor to the most visible leaders, not necessarily the ones who are working hard in the trenches for the Body.

What exactly did Paul mean when he said to give these elders *double honor*? Part of the answer is in verse eighteen, where Paul quoted from the Old Testament, saying, "You don't muzzle an ox while it is treading out the grain." Paul then quoted Jesus by saying that the worker deserved his pay. Part of the honor that was shown to them was a financial gift or provision, but it also was their pay for the work they did in laboring for souls of others (see Heb. 13:17).

What did Paul refer to when he spoke of an ox treading out the grain? He was actually referring to a verse from the Old Testament that taught it was both compassionate and practical to take care of the animals that work for us. Paul was being extremely practical here: we don't neglect the beast of burden that is working for us. If we want them to continue to work and have the energy they need to keep up their productivity, then we must continue to feed them and take care of them. It makes no sense at all to neglect the animal that is working to provide food for the household. Having no oxen meant having no food on our table.

In the same way, when someone is preaching, teaching, and discipling people in the gospel, thereby feeding them spiritual food, we are not to muzzle them. We must care for their practical needs. We provide them with double honor because we are making it possible for them to eat and be healthy so we likewise can eat spiritual food and be spiritually healthy. We are to make it possible for them to eat, to be sustained, and to be well taken care of, because by so doing we will also be taken care of.

Paul instructed another young man. He was named Titus. Paul instructed him to make sure Zenas and Apollos had what they need:

> Make every effort to help Zenas the lawyer and Apollos on their way; *make sure they have what they need.* Here is another way that our people can learn to engage in good works to meet pressing needs and so not be unfruitful. (Titus 3:13–14 NET)

Not only did Paul want Zenas and Apollos taken care of, but he also said that it was a way for people to enter into and demonstrate good works. By funding workers and taking care of pressing needs, the Body of Christ is able to enter into good works that have been prepared for us to walk in. Engaging in providing for the needs of others is actually the antidote for unfruitfulness. When workers and missionaries are properly funded, it causes the Body of Christ to be fruitful while she engages in good works, and it also empowers the worker as the gospel goes forth throughout the earth.

John's Desire to Support Missionaries

Later on in the New Testament, John wrote a letter addressing this same topic, supporting others in the gospel in a manner that is worthy of God. He said:

Dear friend, you demonstrate *faithfulness* by whatever you do for the brothers (even though they are strangers). They have testified to your love before the church. You will do well to *send them on their way in a manner worthy of God.* For they have gone forth on behalf of "The Name," accepting nothing from the pagans. *Therefore we ought to support such people,* so that we become coworkers in cooperation with the truth. (3 Jn. 5–8 NET)

John was writing about a group of people who had been preaching Christ, and who had gone forth in "The Name," meaning the name of Christ. Even though they were strangers, they were still brothers in the Lord. And he told them they would do well to send these people on their way, because it was actually an opportunity to do a good deed unto the Lord.

Faithfulness is demonstrated by caring for the worker/ messenger who is sent out (v. 5). John reminded his readers that they would do well *to send the workers on their way*, which is the Greek word *propempō*. This Greek word means to send someone on a journey, to join them for part of it, or to make sure the person has all he or she needs. So John was essentially saying to put bread in their sack, to put money in their purse, and then send them on their way to continue preaching the gospel—and to do so in a manner worthy of God. The word *propempō* shows up nine times in the New Testament, and when read in context we get the impression that not only is it practical but it's a word of agreement, showing loving assistance and close comradery (see Acts 15:3; 20:38; 21:5; Rom. 15:24; 1 Cor. 16:6, 11; 2 Cor. 1:16; Titus 3:13; 3 Jn. 6ff.).

How do we send a worker on his way in a manner worthy of God? The key is in the Greek word *propempō*. They were to send them in a way that was tender, close, loving, and intimate—a way that was supportive and practical. The Church was to send them on their way as if Jesus Himself were there being sent out. If Jesus were physically present in our midst today, and He had been preaching the gospel to our church, how would we send Him out? Would we give Him everything He needed for His journey—food, money, and other resources? Would we give Him our leftovers or our best? Would we hug Him and pray for Him? The way we would send out Jesus is the way we should send out His workers.

Furthermore, John went on to say that we "ought to support such people." We should rally around these people, give them assistance, making sure they have everything they need, including prayer, friendship, and encouragement as they go out and preach the gospel.

When we support workers, we become coworkers in cooperation with the truth they are sharing. We are actually sharing in the work they are doing when we financially support them. By giving to missionaries who can go, we are coming into agreement with the truth they are sharing, which is the truth of the gospel about Jesus, His coming kingdom, and the restoration of all things. Where our money goes, we go.

What is happening when we partner together with those being sent out is that we are being united together with one another, where goers and senders become acquainted with one another and, through the invitation of financial partnership from the goers, the senders become coworkers with them. Not only can the missionary now go out in strength and do his job, but he can go out with the love, agreement, and support of the people who have sent him out. This is a practical way to engage the Body of Christ in the Great Commission.

God, in His wise leadership, has given us a model that is engaging, practical, empowering, and spiritually healthy. When the Body of Christ works together through partnership, not only does the cause of Christ go forward in strength, but there are spiritual benefits for both goer and sender. Financial partnership is a demonstration of faithfulness (see 3 Jn. 1:5-8). It provides a context for fellowship—*koinōneō* (see 2 Cor. 8:4; Rom. 15:26). The giver earns an eternal reward (see Phil. 4:17). And partnership engages the Body of Christ in good works and produces spiritual fruit (Titus 3:14).

Conclusion

Our perspective and attitude of how the Lord supports His workers must withstand the test of Scripture. We want to move forward in our ministry with a confidence and liberty that comes from the written Word of God, not the standard that is set by our culture or missions traditions. We can see there is a long line of New Testament passages and examples that show the nearly two-thousand-year-old ministry of the people of God funding full-time workers still carries on today. God not only provides the vision to the people of God, but through sharing vision, He stirs the hearts of His people, and they give. Jesus, His disciples, Paul, and John give us powerful examples that funding workers isn't relegated to the Old Testament alone.

Looking Inside

- Jesus had a partnership team that empowered the ministry. How does this affect you looking forward?

- Do you believe that God would give you relationships with a partnership team like He gave Paul?

- Does the thought of interdependence frighten you? Why?

- What do you need to do as a goer or as a sender to step into John's exhortation in Third John 5–8?

Taking Action

1. Spend thirty minutes reading through and meditating on Acts 2:44–45 and Acts 4:32–35.

2. After you have read through the scripture verses a couple of times, then answer the following questions.

   - Do you see a stewardship perspective in these two passages?

   - In verse 34, do you think *anyone* could have included full-time workers?

   - In verse 34, what was made possible by the family of God working together?

   - In the above passage, lack was eliminated, and Second Corinthians 8:14, Ephesians 4:28, and Titus 3:14–15 all encourage giving to eliminate lack. Do you believe God still cares about eliminating lack? How does this apply to the missionary?

CHAPTER SIX

Self-Funding vs. Partnership

Things aren't always as they first appear.

Now that we have reviewed the biblical evidence present in both Testaments of the model for partnership development, we want to investigate two present-day assumptions conflicting with the model. Much of the misunderstanding of how missionaries are supported comes from these two presuppositions: 1) that the apostle Paul's model for funding his ministry was actually self-funding by his being a tentmaker, and 2) that Church tradition's model is not to seek funding but to fulfill missions "living by faith alone." For this chapter, we will be dissecting the first assumption. The second assumption will be thoroughly addressed in the next chapter.

The idea that Paul was a tentmaker and self-funded his ministry doing so has created a culture within missions that expects missionaries to be self-sustaining (i.e., to work a job and minister on the side). This thinking comes from only a couple of verses in the New Testament where Paul says something like, "I worked with my hands in order that I wouldn't be a burden to you or a hindrance to the gospel." We are going to examine some of these verses much more closely in order to find out if Paul really was a tentmaker, and if so, what were the reasons behind his being employed. As we discussed in earlier chapters of part 2, there is a clear history of the saints supporting priests, prophets, New Testament workers, Jesus Himself, His disciples, and the apostles after they were informed of the work and mission of the same. With such a clear history of supporting gospel workers, why was Paul making tents in order to fulfill the call of God?

I have seen this misunderstanding with both the sender and the goer. Missionaries, thinking they have to work a job or create a business, often become so distracted by it that they end up doing very little ministry at all. Sometimes, it is the sender who has this misunderstanding and never gives, expecting the missionary to be self-supported. I saw this common misunderstanding play out recently with a missionary friend who was in a season of partnership development. He had shared a letter with a friend and asked for an opportunity to share with him face-to-face. In the meeting, my missionary friend invited his friend to be a financial partner in ministry. The potential partner's response was, "Hey, I have a support raising idea for you—you can clean my house, and I will pay you."

My missionary friend said, "That's not partnership—that's a job. And I already have a job. No thank you."

Even though it is assumed Paul made tents throughout the entirety of his ministry, that was simply not the case. Paul only made tents on three occasions in his thirty-plus years of ministry. He made tents while ministering at Ephesus, for a period of about three years; while at Corinth, which was about eighteen months (he didn't make tents the whole time he was there); and then at Thessalonica, which most scholars agree was only for a couple of months. First, let's look at his time at Thessalonica, and then we will go back to his times at Corinth and Ephesus.

Paul at Thessalonica

Because of intense persecution and an overall tension, Paul stayed in Thessalonica only for a short time. We know he was there for at least three weeks, but most scholars agree that it would have been more like two or three months. It is possible that sufficient time had not passed for Paul to build mature relationships with the people there who could support him.

Paul was also dealing with a number of accusations that had come against him in those few weeks: two of them being that he was greedy and lazy, which probably came from persecuting Jews. A number of the Thessalonians had become quite idle themselves. In both letters to Thessalonica, Paul stated that he took care of himself, ensuring he was a burden to no one. In the second letter, he presented himself as an example for the idle—of what they should do. And it was primarily for that reason Paul worked with his hands, resulting in his writing:

> For even when we were with you, we commanded you this: If anyone will not work, neither shall he eat. For we hear that there are some who walk among you in a disorderly manner, not working at all, but are busybodies. Now those who are such we command and exhort through our Lord Jesus Christ that they work in quietness and eat their own bread. (2 Thes. 3:10–12)

Paul wasn't working because he needed to; he was working to give the idle an example that they should "work in quietness" and provide for themselves. It is also important to keep in mind the following verse:

> And as you Philippians know, at the beginning of my gospel ministry, when I left Macedonia, no church shared with me in this matter of giving and receiving except you alone. *For even in Thessalonica on more than one occasion you sent something for my need.* (Phil. 4:15–16 NET)

While Paul "worked with his hands" at Thessalonica, the church at Philippi was supporting him. Paul wasn't tentmaking because he thought it to be the best model for raising missions support or because he needed the money. Actually, he was receiving support from the Philippians, so he was trying to address bad behavior at Thessalonica and knew it would be best for him to demonstrate the right behavior. His tentmaking wasn't related to self-funding his mission work.

Defending His Apostleship

The key to understanding First and Second Corinthians is in realizing the tension that existed in the church because of the presence of false Jewish apostles. They claimed to be men of God but constantly challenged Paul and Barnabas in their true apostleship. These false apostles endeavored to bring down the true apostles by discrediting them. They wanted to win over the people of Corinth and lure them away. It was their intention to get the church at Corinth to be faithful to them instead of to Paul and Barnabas.

This tension surfaced in Paul's letters several times, where we see him defend his apostleship. But in defending his apostleship, he actually talked about the issue of provision and financial support. He wrote to the Corinthians:

> Am I not free? Am I not an apostle? Have I not seen Jesus our Lord? Are you not my work in the Lord? If I am not an apostle to others, at least I am to you, for you are the confirming sign of my apostleship in the Lord. (1 Cor. 9:1–2 NET)

If Paul wasn't an apostle to anyone else, he certainly was to the church at Corinth. They were a church because of his ministry among them, his having established the church at Corinth.

> Then Paul gave his defense for his apostleship:
> *This is my defense to those who examine me.* Do we not have the right to financial support? Do we not have the right to the company of a believing wife, like the other apostles and the Lord's brothers and Cephas? Or do only Barnabas and I lack the right not to work? (1 Cor. 9:3–6 NET)

The first thing he asked was: "Do we not have the right to financial support?" The other apostles throughout the early church were married and were being financially supported, but Paul and Barnabas were not. Paul uses the word *right* (it means freedom) three times in verses five through seven: did he not have the *right* to financial support, did he not have the *right* to have the company of a believing wife, and did he not have the *right not* to work and be fully supported by the gospel? As a worker, yes, he had the right. However, he chose not to receive support from the Corinthian church. Why? Well, we will answer that question a little later.

To make his point even further, he appealed to their common sense and the Law. He wrote:

Who ever serves in the army at his own expense? Who plants a vineyard and does not eat its fruit? Who tends a flock and does not consume its milk? Am I saying these things only on the basis of common sense, or does the law not say this as well? (1 Cor. 9:7–8 NET)

Paul compared his apostleship to three natural examples: an army, a vineyard, and a flock. He said that every worker who sows or serves does so with an expectation of a return. No one joins an army and then pays himself for serving in that army. No one plants a vineyard and doesn't have the right to eat and drink from it. The fact that the vineyard is owned by someone suggests that person gets to reap benefits from it. Likewise, everyone who owns a flock gets to benefit from the production of that flock.

Next, Paul turned to the Law:

For it is written in the law of Moses, "Do not muzzle an ox while it is treading out the grain." God is not concerned here about oxen, is he? Or is he not surely speaking for our benefit? It was written for us, because the one plowing and threshing ought to work in hope of enjoying the harvest. (1 Cor. 9:9–10 NET)

The Old Testament command to not muzzle the ox was both compassionate and practical. It would be cruel to not properly feed and care for animals. And if the ox were not taken care of, eventually it would be so weak it would not be able to work, resulting in the owner not having any grain to eat.

Paul made a clear statement in verse 11: "If we sowed spiritual blessings among you, is it too much to reap material things from you?" Paul was in the army of God, he was a worker in God's vineyard, and he was a shepherd over the Corinthians. If he had sown spiritual blessings among them, he said it would be his right to reap material things from them. But he was not done with his defense, so he continued:

> If others receive this right from you, are we not more deserving? But we have not made use of this right. Instead we endure everything so that we may not be a hindrance to the gospel of Christ. (1 Cor. 9:12 NET)

It is often taught that Paul didn't receive any financial support from the church of Corinth because that would have put a financial burden on the church there. And, as being a burden on the church, they wouldn't have been able to preach as effectively, and somehow the gospel of Christ would be hindered. But this is not true.

We know that the church at Corinth was supporting other apostles during this time. That is why Paul said, "If others receive this right from you, are we not more deserving?" How would giving and receiving support, which Paul said was good and fruitful, hinder the gospel going forth to the Corinthians? How would giving to God and His missional purpose be a burden?

Let's see what Paul said:

Don't you know that those who serve in the temple eat
food from the temple, and those who serve at the altar
receive a part of the offerings? *In the same way the Lord
commanded those who proclaim the gospel to receive
their living by the gospel.* (1 Cor. 9:13–14 NET)

Paul referenced Leviticus 7 in these verses, and it outlined the way
the priests were to eat of the sacrifices brought to the temple. That
is what Paul called attention to here.[1] The offering that was given
to God was partly consumed by the priest when it was given. So
by referencing Leviticus 7, Paul showed that his apostolic ministry
was as legitimate and worthy of support as the priesthood and that
supporting him would not be doing anything new; it would only
be doing what had been previously done in the past—for almost
two thousand years.

Now, when Paul said, "*In the same way* the Lord commanded
those who proclaim the gospel to receive their living by the gospel,"
he was making a strong statement. "Commanded" is a good translation from the original Greek word. Paul recognized that the Lord
had not merely recommended those who proclaim the gospel to
receive their living by it, nor did He suggest it. The apostle said
that the Lord commanded! Paul followed the instructions of Jesus
and here in First Corinthians was most likely referring to Matthew
10:10 and Luke 10:7.

But I have not used any of these rights. And I am not writing these things so that something will be done for me.
In fact, it would be better for me to die than—no one will
deprive me of my reason for boasting! (1 Cor. 9:15 NET)

Paul did obey Jesus' instructions in the command to be supported by the gospel. He did it all throughout his thirty-plus years of ministry; he was just not doing it here with the Corinthians even though he received support from other churches while ministering to Corinth.

Paul made it clear that he was entitled to financial support, but he had a reason to boast and wanted to maintain his boast. In other words, he wanted to clearly say, "I'm not in it for the money. I'm in it for you!"

Then he said:

For if I preach the gospel, I have no reason for boasting, because I am compelled to do this. Woe to me if I do not preach the gospel! For if I do this voluntarily, I have a reward. But if I do it unwillingly, I am entrusted with a responsibility. What then is my reward? That when I preach the gospel I may offer the gospel free of charge, and so not make full use of my rights in the gospel. (1 Cor. 9:16–18 NET)

Paul understood that he had been called to preach the gospel, he was going to do it, and he would do it willingly and receive a reward for it. At any point of his ministry, if Paul were to make preaching the gospel dependent upon pay, then he would not receive a reward for preaching voluntarily, although he did have a right to be supported and should be supported. If Paul had made the issue of financial support a deal-breaker, walking away from the church at Corinth, not only would he have lost his reward, but then who then would be left to minister to the Corinthians? They would only have had the false apostles. This is critical to our understanding what Paul meant in the "big picture."

In response to being accused that he was only being an apostle for financial gain, Paul chose not to receive financial support from the Corinthians in order to set himself apart from the false apostles, demonstrating that he had a genuine love for the church at Corinth and was not in it for money. Once again, Paul did something that from a quick glance at the biblical text seemed to support the model of self-funding; however, when we look into the context and see the backstory, as it were, we realize he was not presenting self-funding as a model.

Paul had a right to be supported. After all, it makes sense in the natural realm, it is written in the Law, it is in the spirit of Leviticus 7, and it is the very thing the Lord Jesus commanded.

Paul's Second Address to Corinth

In his second letter to the church at Corinth, Paul brought up the issue once again, saying that he robbed other churches in order to bring the gospel to them:

Indeed, I consider that I am not in the least inferior to these super-apostles. Even if I am unskilled in speaking, I am not so in knowledge; indeed, in every way we have made this plain to you in all things. Or did I commit a sin in humbling myself so that you might be exalted, because I preached God's gospel to you free of charge? *I robbed other churches by accepting support from them in order to serve you.* And when I was with you and was in need, I did not burden anyone, for the brothers who came from Macedonia supplied my need. So I refrained and will refrain from burdening you in any way. (2 Cor. 11:5–9 ESV)

So Paul received financial support from other churches, and by receiving support from those churches, he was better able to serve the church at Corinth. Paul was not suggesting that he stole money from other churches, but he simply meant that his not taking money from the Corinthians but instead being supported by other churches was to show the Corinthians he was not in it for financial gain and truly loved them. Paul may have been referring to Acts 18.

In Acts 18, Paul left Athens and made his way to Corinth. Upon arriving there, he found a Jew named Aquila and his wife Priscilla, who were there because they had been kicked out of Rome. He discovered they were tentmakers, so he stayed with them for a time:

And he was reasoning in the synagogue every Sabbath and trying to persuade Jews and Greeks. But when Silas and Timothy came down from Macedonia, Paul *began devoting himself completely to the word*, solemnly testifying to the Jews that Jesus was the Christ. (Acts 18:4–5 NASB)

Paul made tents all week and then would reason with the Jews once a week on the Sabbath. But when Silas and Timothy came down from Macedonia, Paul stopped tentmaking and began devoting himself completely to the work. In the midst of the tension that was in Corinth, Paul supported himself and thereby set himself apart from the false apostles there. But when the brothers came (they must have brought financial gifts or Paul would have kept making tents), Paul immediately devoted himself completely to the Word. Paul's tentmaking took a lot of time and energy, leaving him to contend once a week on the Sabbath. When the financial support came in, however, he then shifted his time and energy and started devoting himself entirely to the work. In this case, Paul's tentmaking actually took away from the ministry, leaving him only with enough time and energy to minister once a week.

This is a dynamic I see all too often, a worker called to full-time ministry doing whatever he or she can to make it work, but the secular employment pulls the worker away from God's assignment. The missionaries I talk to often feel like failures because the work isn't getting done and they are tired and still broke. It doesn't have to be this way. God intends for us to work together, everyone playing his or her role, either as the goer or the sender. There is a high price to pay for called, full-time occupational ministers trying to support themselves through marketplace jobs. Like Paul, the twenty or thirty hours of labor in the marketplace doesn't afford the worker the time necessary to focus on the Word and the mission.

Looking once again to Second Corinthians 11, Paul said:
As the truth of Christ is in me, this boasting of mine will not be silenced in the regions of Achaia. And why? Because I do not love you? God knows I do! *And what I am doing I will continue to do, in order to undermine the claim of those who would like to claim that in their boasted mission they work on the same terms as we do.* (vv. 10–12 ESV)

Paul and Barnabas drew a contrast between themselves and the false apostles. So Paul was essentially saying, "I've been with you, entitled to financial support, but I didn't insist on having that right." And he said he would continue to do this to undermine the claim of the false apostles who would like the Corinthians to think that Paul and Barnabas were only in it for the money. They provided for themselves and laid down their financial rights in order to serve out of love. Paul was saying, "I love. These false apostles do not."

> For such men are false apostles, deceitful workmen, disguising themselves as apostles of Christ. And no wonder, for even Satan disguises himself as an angel of light. So it is no surprise if his servants, also, disguise themselves as servants of righteousness. Their end will correspond to their deeds. (2 Cor. 11:13–15 ESV)

Paul's strong words underscore the seriousness of the situation at Corinth. These alleged apostles were not brothers who were a little off in their thinking or maybe had bad attitudes. No, these men had evil intent!

The idea that Paul was a committed, self-supported tentmaker isn't an accurate picture. Whenever he entered into ministry, he entered into this dynamic of giving and receiving, just like he did with the church in Philippi. Paul was only operating in the same pattern everyone else had operated in since the establishment of the priesthood in Exodus. His goal was to prove his love and his true apostleship by differentiating himself from crooked and evil men.

Paul's Repentance for Wronging the Corinthians

Paul was again accused of being harsh and of mistreating the Corinthians. In response to this, he wrote in his second letter: "For how were you treated worse than the other churches, except that I myself was not a burden to you? Forgive me this injustice!" (2 Cor. 12:13 NET). (See 2 Cor. 12:12–18 in order to see this verse in its context). Many other translations end this statement with, "Forgive me of this wrong!"

Paul is repenting of not allowing the Corinthians to support him. Some would suggest Paul was being sarcastic here, but I believe he was being sincere. Corinthian believers were charging him with not treating them the same way he had treated others, which was true. Paul had been supported by many churches for many years. He was in partnership with the Philippians over the years, but he had not allowed the church at Corinth to support him. I believe this tenderhearted apostle actually regretted the decision he had made while he was with them, calling his own action an "injustice." He really apologized for not allowing the Corinthians the same opportunity he allowed others—and that was to give toward the mission.

I believe Paul was hoping to change the situation at Corinth, and he was hoping to win them with his sincerity by not "burdening" them. In the end, it seemed as though there was no change. Either way, whether he was being sarcastic or literal, it doesn't change much of what took place here. Paul had clearly communicated that as a worker he was entitled to financial support.

Paul at Ephesus

Finally, when we investigate the time Paul spent tentmaking at Ephesus, we discover Paul didn't say much about the reason he did so there. However, we can glean a little about the situation from Acts 20:29–35. From this passage of Scripture, we know that the condition at Ephesus was not completely unlike the situation at Corinth.

In verses twenty-nine and thirty, Paul said that wolves were going to come in after his departure, men from their own group, who would teach perversions in order to draw disciples unto themselves. In verse thirty-one, Paul reminded them that, for three years, he had warned them night and day with tears. Paul used verses thirty-three through thirty-five to remind them that he did not desire their gold and silver but that he had worked with his hands to provide for his needs and by doing so modeled how they must work in order to help the needy. This sounds very similar to what he said in Thessalonica, where he was demonstrating to others how to conduct themselves.

One thing we know for sure is that Paul was not against receiving support. He was also not putting his tentmaking forward as the chosen model for his livelihood. Paul made it clear that a worker is worthy of support. He even spoke about the rights of a worker like himself to receive supply from brothers and sisters in Christ.

The idea that missionaries have to be tentmakers is so well-established in our society that it permeates the whole missions movement. It has made many feel as if they have no other option but to work full-time and then try to minister with the leftover time they have. But all of this stems from a misunderstanding of a few references to Paul's being a tentmaker.

Conclusion

Scripture does not require the worker to fund himself or herself in ministry; in reality, the opposite is true. The priest didn't do it in the Old Testament, Jesus didn't do it in the New Testament, and, for most of his ministry, Paul didn't do it either. Several positive biblical principles are diminished when we require ourselves and others to be self-funded "tentmakers"; namely, fruitfulness, good deeds, co-laboring, eternal reward, and cooperating with truth.

The more we work outside of our calling, the less we enter into giving and receiving and interdependence within the family of God. There are many issues in our own hearts that can only be dealt with when we enter into that close relationship of interdependence with other saints in the Body of Christ.

In some situations, tentmaking is the open door for ministry in closed countries. Missionaries use their jobs for access and, sometimes, as a means for ministry service. I say yes and amen to them! There is a place and time for tentmaking. Sometimes the situation requires it, and in many cases it is the wisest way to get the gospel to people. So do whatever we can do in order to get the gospel into regions that are closed off to the gospel.

Many may think that tentmaking is their only option. However, I would encourage them to wholeheartedly seek the Lord on this issue. If we are called to full-time ministry, we need to believe that a worker is worthy of his wages, operate in the freedom and expectation of Scripture, and know that God has a support team for us.

Looking Inside

- In Western culture, why does tentmaking mostly apply to missionaries and not the local church?

- Besides Paul, who is another example of a full-time minister who supported himself/herself with a tentmaking job in the Bible? Can you think of one?

- If Jesus had been a tentmaker, and His ministry was reduced as a result, what would the Gospels look like?

- If you could devote 100 percent of your time to ministry, in what way could you serve the Lord that you currently aren't able to because of your tentmaking?

- If you have been or plan to be a self-funded missionary, what's influencing you—Scripture, tradition, fear, or the culture?

Taking Action

1. Find one tentmaking missionary and ask him or her these questions: "How much time do you spend making tents? And, if that time was free to serve within your assignment, what more could you do?"

2. Look at your own life. Ask yourself the same questions and write down a list of ministry things you could do if your time was free to do them.

CHAPTER SEVEN

Living by Faith Alone?

Prayer without the use of means, where means can be employed, is a new doctrine.
–Frank F. Ellinwood[1]

Our perspectives and attitudes about how the Lord supports His full-time occupational workers must withstand the test of Scripture. We want to move forward in our ministry with a confidence that comes from the written Word of God, not by what is dictated to us by missions tradition or our current culture. Is the "faith missions," the "through prayer alone," or "living by faith alone" approach—that is, just believe, go, pray, tell only God about our needs and then somehow the money will find us—the model of Scripture? Furthermore, what is biblical faith, and what role does it have for the full-time worker?

Historically, in missions circles, it has not been uncommon to hear the phrases "faith missions" or "living by faith alone" or even "by no means but through prayer" when it comes to serving God on the mission field. When many missionaries use these phrases, it generally means they do not have predictable financial resources and are not planning to talk with anyone about financial support before beginning their mission or later during the mission. Often, it's a pledge to never talk about money or current needs. They say, "God knows my needs; therefore, I will tell no one but God and trust Him alone to meet my needs."

This model has been around since the early 1800s, though it has ebbed and flowed in popularity and practice since that time. Some of the testimonies from this approach can be very inspiring, but for the overwhelming majority, this approach has led to considerable heartache, marital stress, disillusionment, dashed dreams, and incomplete assignments—ministry that never began. These are testimonies that we never hear because they are never shared.

But like any model, it must withstand the test of Scripture. Does this model of tell no one but God and go only on faith withstand that test? If it were a biblical model, then its pattern and the people represented by it must be well documented throughout the Bible. Is this the case?

In asking these questions, I am not wanting to rob any individuals of their traditions or histories. I am not looking to do away with the incredible testimonies of how saints have personally exercised their faith in the annals of Church history. I do not want to rob anyone of their own experience or the history of their movement's founders. My goal is to allow the Scriptures to speak to us regarding the means God uses to provide for His servants in their fulfilling His mission and, in so doing, free us all to walk in the liberty the Scriptures grant us.

In the multiple trainings that I have conducted, I have asked missionaries about their understanding of the "living by faith alone" practice, what it means, or how they would define it. I have also asked for them to give me a scriptural basis for this model. Without fail, whenever I have pressed them to give me a scriptural example and definition, the first words out of their mouths were almost always a particular saint's testimony from the past, which I acknowledge and appreciate.

Most generally, however, when I press them further, they will give me two or three other figures from the history of missions. But when I ask them again for scriptural support, then they usually give me one of three Scripture passages: Matthew 10 or Luke 9, about Jesus' sending out the Twelve; First Kings 17, where the ravens fed Elijah during a drought; and Matthew 6, about how God feeds the birds of the air and provides for their needs. We are going to take a look at these three passages and see if the model of "living by faith alone" withstands the test of Scripture.

Sending out the Disciples

Matthew 10 and Luke 9 are parallel passages of Jesus' sending out the twelve disciples. In chapter 5, we looked at Matthew 10, so there is no need to cover it again in detail here. However, suffice it to say that Jesus' sending out the Twelve in the manner He did was not a commission of some sort of super faith where He said something like, "Trust Me, and you'll have everything you need." But as they were commanded to heal the sick, raise the dead, and preach the gospel, the twelve disciples were also commanded to find those who were worthy in the city with whom they could share their vision.

The question becomes for us, how do we find out who is worthy? Those who are worthy are those who have ears to hear. Also, the command given by Jesus goes on to state that, when they found someone who was worthy, they were to stay with that person in his or her house. There is a connection between those who are worthy, those who have ears to hear, and provision.

Matthew 10 and Luke 9 are encouraging and specific instructions, but they are not an adequate basis for the "living by faith alone" model. The disciples did not head out not knowing how they were going to be provided for; in fact, they knew exactly how they were going to be taken care of. They were to share their vision with others, and those who had ears to hear would attend to their needs. In other words, they did not practice the "living by faith alone" model by not telling anyone but God about their mission or vision. They did trust their heavenly Father, and they did believe, but they also obeyed what Jesus told them to do. The Twelve went, they shared, and others had ears to hear and met the disciples' needs.

Another reason we know that this is not the primary model for missions is because Jesus did not follow the model. It is important to note that, even as Jesus commanded the disciples how they were to travel, He Himself was properly funded and fully clothed; in fact, His ministry had a treasurer by the name of Judas and a bag in which all the money was held. Jesus' model was not a model of "going without" or going "by faith alone." No, His model was going without being "self-funded." Jesus told them to leave *their* things at home for a worker was worthy of a wage. So when the disciples shared their vision and the hearts of the hearers were stirred, the giving of those hearers—their sharing their homes and hospitality with the disciples—was the provision from the Lord. The Twelve, then, knew where they would get their supply, though they did not know the specific persons who would help them. And they knew this all before they ever obeyed Jesus' words to actually go.

Commanding Ravens

Elijah, too, had an understanding how God was going to meet his needs. He called down a drought on the land of Israel, saying that it was not going to rain for the next few years except by his word (1 Kgs. 17:1). Then the Lord responded to him, telling Elijah to leave that place and go to a particular brook. There, he would drink from the brook, and the ravens would feed him as God had commanded them (1 Kgs. 17:2–4).

Before Elijah ever left to go to the brook, the Lord had revealed to him that He would attend to him at the brook and how He would do so. Elijah wasn't going by faith alone; rather, God specifically told Him to go and drink from a certain brook, and the ravens would feed him there. Elijah knew where his provision was going to come from before he ever obeyed God's word to go.

I am not suggesting that Elijah was not a man of faith—for we can see throughout his ministry that he actually was. The Lord was not responding to Elijah's faith here, though. It required faith on Elijah's part to obey the word of the Lord, as all obedience does. But he did not head out without knowing where his provision was going to come from, as several of the proponents of the "living by faith alone" model purport. No, Elijah knew exactly where and how it would be supplied.

There is also no indication that Elijah prayed in the support. In fact, he had not prayed about his provision at all at that point; he simply responded to the known word of the Lord at the moment. It happened just as the Lord said it would, and we see that Elijah drank from the brook and that the ravens brought him food every day. So he was sustained for a time (1 Kgs. 17:6–8).

When the brook dried up (because of the drought), the Lord then told him to get up and go to Zarephath, for there was a widow in that place who He had commanded to meet Elijah's needs. In the same way the Lord spoke to him about how He was going to sustain him at the brook by the ravens, before he ever left the brook to go to Zarephath, Elijah knew exactly where his provision would come from.

Again, there is no indication from this passage that Elijah prayed in his supply. The Lord came through for him. He provided for Elijah and told him how he would be taken care of. This was no mystery. Elijah went to Zarephath and encountered the widow. The Bible says that the widow was almost completely out of food and she was in the process of gathering a few sticks to cook her and her son's last meal. Elijah told her not to fear, but she was to first make a cake for him and then afterward for herself and her son. Elijah then prophesied to her that, during the period of the drought, she would have enough, that her oil and flour would not run out. With this assurance, she obeyed what he told her. And Elijah's word was true—she did not run out.

This was definitely a miracle, it was definitely provision, and it certainly required faith. However, it is hard to create a case for "living by faith alone," as it is commonly understood within mission circles today. Elijah wasn't launching out on a lifelong journey of service not knowing how he was going to be provided for. He was simply following very specific instructions from the Lord about where to go and how he was going to be cared for during the drought. There is no indication that the Lord was responding to Elijah's faith, although it did require faith to respond to the Lord in both of these situations.

Most scholars agree that the time Elijah was by the brook and ravens were feeding him there was probably no more than six to eight weeks in length. This is hardly sufficient time to establish a model of provision as a full-time worker. And as we read about the life of Elijah, it is easy to see that he was provided for in many different ways. Ravens did not feed him for thirty years of ministry; it was only a couple of months out of decades of his ministry. In all the passages speaking about funding workers in the Great Commission, Elijah is never referred to as the model of how workers are to be sustained. His being fed by the ravens is an extremely encouraging miracle, but it's not really a good basis for the "living by faith alone" model of ministry.

Caring for the Birds of the Air

Matthew 6 is often referred to as the scriptural basis for the "living by faith alone" approach for missions. But it's important to note that Matthew 6:25–34 is right in the middle of Jesus'

Sermon on the Mount (see Mt. 5–7), which is addressed to the multitudes (for every believer), not specifically to missionaries or full-time workers.

In the proceeding verses, Jesus addressed our worldview and made the statement that we cannot serve two masters, for we will either "hate the one and love the other," or "be loyal to the one and despise the other" (Mt. 6:24). We cannot serve both God and mammon. Immediately following this about money and provision, Jesus spoke about the issue of worry. Specifically, Jesus talked about worry in the context of provision, quickly turning His attention to God's care of creation. He said:

> "Therefore I say to you, do not worry about your life, what you will eat or what you will drink; nor about your body, what you will put on. Is not life more than food and the body more than clothing? Look at the birds of the air, for they neither sow nor reap nor gather into barns; yet your heavenly Father feeds them. Are you not of more value than they? Which of you by worrying can add one cubit to his stature? So why do you worry about clothing? Consider the lilies of the field, how they grow: they neither toil nor spin; and yet I say to you that even Solomon in all his glory was not arrayed like one of these. Now if God so clothes the grass of the field, which today is, and tomorrow is thrown into the oven, *will He* not much more *clothe* you, O you of little faith?" (vv. 25–30)

The birds are not like farmers who store up their food in barns, yet according to Jesus' words, the birds are taken care of. Then He makes a similar statement about clothing, using the flowers of the field to make His point. The flowers in the field do not strive or labor, but the Lord has clothed them, and clothed them well, even better than Solomon was arrayed in royal splendor. These flowers are going to die and then be thrown into the fire, and yet God takes the time to clothe them each and every day. God loves us much more than the flowers, so surely He will clothe us and provide for our basic necessities. Worrying about food or other basic necessities in life is not going to add one minute to our lives. So we can understand that the rebuke is for our *not believing* in God's consistent commitment toward us.

Jesus made His concluding remarks by saying that the Gentiles worry about these kinds of things; they do not have the assurance of a heavenly Father who will care for them. But as believers, we should not be worrying about such things, for we can take comfort in the knowledge that God will provide for us:

"Therefore do not worry, saying, 'What shall we eat?' or 'What shall we drink?' or 'What shall we wear?' For after all these things the Gentiles seek. For your heavenly Father knows that you need all these things." (vv. 31–32)

The key to Jesus' teaching is that we should first seek the kingdom of God and His righteousness. When our focus is in the right place and on the right thing, worry becomes a non-issue. Besides, it will get us nowhere and will not add anything to our lives. A proper focus, as Jesus taught, will have its reward:

"But seek first the kingdom of God and His righteousness, and all these things shall be added to you. Therefore do not worry about tomorrow, for tomorrow will worry about its own things. Sufficient for the day is its own trouble." (Mt. 6:33–34)

However, this portion of Jesus' message is not about how to fund workers in the Great Commission, but I can see where it could be easy to conclude that, if we really are not to worry and we really trust in the Lord, then He will simply take care of us. And, in truth, He will and does take care of us. But trusting in the Lord does not mean that we do not engage in His work, that we do not do work, or that we do not have a part to play in seeing His mission go forth in the earth today. No, we have stuff to do, that's for sure. Let me explain using two examples, one Jesus used in His sermon and another I think is appropriate.

When we consider the birds of the air that Jesus mentioned, without question, we understand the Lord provides for them. But how does He do it? He does it in many different ways. He provides grass, mud, sticks, and building materials from which the bird can build its nest. He also supplies insects, worms, seeds, and every type of food for the bird to eat. The Lord bestows everything a bird needs for life, but the bird actually has to go gather its provision every day. At no time does the Lord build a nest for the bird, and at no time does the Lord hand-deliver a worm to the bird. The only time a worm is brought to a bird is when the bird is a baby lacking maturity, the ability and skill to gather for itself—and even at that it is the adult birds that do the work so the baby bird can eat.

In a manner of speaking, the bird is actually acting in faith when it goes out to gather its food. It cannot see the worm, but it knows that the worm (provision) is there. It has seen its Creator provide way too many times to doubt. The bird understands its role and understands it has a part to play. So the bird scratches and pecks around until it finds provision. This is not a lack of faith; it's actually faith in action.

God is going to provide for us, and we do not have to worry about how that provision is going to come. But the Lord provides for us when we participate, cooperate, and partner with Him in what He has called us to do. We must do our part in gathering the Lord's provision. As I explained at the outset of this book, we must lift the lid. We cannot create the provision; we can only gather it.

Now, let's consider a farmer for our second example. A farmer cannot farm properly by sitting in his kitchen and just trusting his farm to the Lord; he must work in partnership with the Lord. A farmer must go out to the field and plow the ground before planting seed. He cannot make that ground fertile, for that part belongs solely to the Lord. A farmer must be the one to plant the seed in the ground, although he cannot create the seed—that's God's part. Then a farmer has to patiently wait. The Lord enters into that process of germination, and in time, that seed breaks open and breaks through the ground. A farmer has to believe God for rain, for he himself cannot make it rain. The Lord is faithful to provide it. Then the Lord has to provide the right amount of light and the right temperature, and then He protects the crop from insects.

When that crop comes to full maturity, the Lord will not go into that field and harvest the crop for the farmer; rather, a farmer has to do it, and it is very hard work. Once that crop is harvested, then that farmer has to take that crop to market and trust God for a good price. When a farmer and the Lord work together in partnership, and when the end of harvest comes, he will sit down, put his feet up, and rest by the fire, saying that the Lord has taken very good care of him. But make no mistake, a farmer had to do his part.

Matthew 6:25–34 is encouraging and should assure us that, if we do our part, God will do His part, and together we will have all the provision we need. Matthew 6, Matthew 10 and Luke 9, and First Kings 17 are encouraging stories, but they are not a biblical basis for the "living by faith alone" approach that is commonly embraced in missions today. We do need faith for our provision, but we need a biblical faith that understands our own role and takes action to partner with the Lord. We do need to obey, we do need to understand where our provision is at, and we need to get up and engage and gather what God has stored up for us.

Faith to Partner with God

Our definition of faith must be the same for all situations, in every time period in history, with every demographic and every culture. There cannot be a definition of faith for the missionary and another definition for all the other believers. There is only one definition of faith for all who believe. I have witnessed those who have the "living by faith alone" model only apply it to missionaries; that is to say, that missionaries are required to trust God for provision while all other Christians are expected to apply for jobs, create résumés, do interviews, develop products, find clients, and make sales. Most pastors in the West are not expected to live by the "faith alone" model, for they typically know what their salary is going to be and where it is going to come from, and rightfully so.

A definition of faith that only applies to missionaries is not really a good definition of faith at all.

This model, as it is currently understood in some missions circles, is not demonstrated by anyone in Scripture. Jesus Himself had a partnership team, and the Old Testament priests knew how they were to be provided for. Paul worked with partnership teams, writing letters asking for financial assistance and encouraging others to assist the missionaries that he was sending to them. Our model for how missionaries are funded must withstand the test of Scripture. In the Word of God, what we repeatedly see happening within the Body of Christ are saints gathering around other saints, vision being communicated, and partnerships forming for prayer, financial support, and material support. God's job is to provide for our needs, but our job is to gather that provision.

Some friends of mine who had been in ministry for almost twenty years, living by faith, which really meant they had to get speaking engagements to pay the bills, were starting to have serious struggles. They were not being invited to speak as much, and at their current later stage of life, the cost of living was getting higher. They wound up with some serious debt, no money, and no way to pay the bills.

They knew the Lord had called them, but they were confused by the situation, a bit ashamed by it, and just tired of the constant struggle. In desperation to obey God, they came to me and asked me for advice. I spoke to them about building a financial partnership team. At first they were not open to the idea, but their strong desire to serve the Lord prevailed, and they began to meet with me.

After only a few sessions, they could see that the "living by faith alone" model lacked scriptural support and that financial partnership was well-documented in Scripture. They began to build a team of financial partners, and in about nine months' time, they paid off all their debts, had a stable income, and were able to give more. Most notably, for the first time in their lives, they were able to save a little money. They are currently serving full-time and are full of joy.

Conclusion

The model of "living by faith alone" lacks a scriptural foundation. The three passages shared in this chapter are not about how to fund workers and they don't lay a good foundation for the faith alone approach. There isn't one full-time worker in the Bible who used this model throughout their years of ministry.

Secondly, this model doesn't empower the worker, making them fully available for years of service, and it doesn't strengthen the Great Commission. Jesus said we need workers for the harvest, and that those workers are worthy of a wage. Rather, this model puts a restriction on workers that Scripture does not. Instead of their being free to find partners for the promulgation of the gospel, they wait alone in their need until . . . until God decides to provide by the ravens or the kindness of strangers. I do not mean to demean or belittle anyone who wants to trust God for His miraculous provision, but scripturally speaking, God is into bringing together brothers and sisters in the Body to work together with Him, every joint or member supplying for the other (Eph. 4:16).

Using this model puts *all* the responsibility and burden on the worker and does not engage the Body of Christ in its stewardship responsibility within the Great Commission. The partnership between goer and sender is to be equal. Remember our definition here: *two separate but equal parties, with separate but equal responsibilities, working together to achieve a common goal.*

When the "living by faith alone" model does not work, when its workers have to return from their missions because there is no miraculous provision, the workers are unjustly charged with a lack of faith. This, in turn, can make them question whether or not they really heard from the Lord in the first place. This has led to a great deal of shame and condemnation that is truly unfair. That missionary had enough faith to say yes to God, enough faith to move to a foreign country, but not enough faith to be provided for? Really? A lack of faith as the source of problems is more than most can bear. Finally, emotionally unable to live with the charge of not having enough faith, they will rewrite the assignment, reducing it until it can be achieved with almost no resource at all. Or they rewrite it so that it will read something like, "The grace has lifted; the Lord is transitioning us back to the marketplace."

The "living by faith alone" approach, as noble as it sounds, is unnecessarily restrictive and emotionally hard on the worker. It robs the Body of Christ of the spiritual healthiness and fruit of partnership, as well as weakens the worker and denying the Great Commission the labor force it needs to be fulfilled. I mean no harm to those saints who have believed for the miraculous and have received a great blessing from the Lord. I do not want to rob anyone of their own experience or history in God, but I believe the "living by faith alone" motto has hindered missions far more than it has empowered it, for I have seen many who have been sidelined or whose mission has been run aground by it.

Our definition of faith must come from the Scriptures, and it must be a definition that applies to every believer, in every culture, and in every time period of history. It cannot be a faith based on occupation, culture, situation, or circumstance.

The Word of God established a precedent of partnership where individuals are not to go it alone. They are neither self-funded nor restricted in their gathering together a team to steward God's resources for the mission. And when we gain this understanding, we are liberated to move into sharing His vision with others whose hearts He will stir to participate in the harvest.

Looking Inside

- I want to encourage you before you consider the questions below. If you have been trying to operate under the heavy yoke of "by faith alone," then look closely at the Scriptures for yourself. They actually free you to invite the Body of Christ to co-labor with you. When you walk in the freedom of the Word of God, then you are free to walk in the strength of team ministry.

- Is a "living by faith alone" expectation holding you back from building a partnership team?

- In your opinion, is faith passive or proactive?

- We prove faith by works. If you believe the Lord has called you to ministry and is going to provide for you, what are the works that you need to do?

- When Paul asked for assistance in Romans 15:24, was it an act of faith?

- Are any other workers expected to go by faith alone, other than missionaries?

Taking Action

1. Take thirty minutes and read Second Kings 4:1–7. Slowly read the passage a couple of times.

2. Answer the following questions about the reading.

   - Who are all the characters involved in this miracle? (There are five.)

   - When the woman cries out to Elisha, is it a cry of faith?

   - When the widow and her sons obeyed the word of the prophet, was that obedience in faith?

   - Is asking the neighbors for vessels presumptuous, a work of the flesh, or an act of trusting God?

   - When God starts pouring the oil, is He responding to their faith or just acting mercifully?

   - Was the widow's faith passive or active?

PART THREE:
A MODERN APPLICATION
OF BIBLICAL PARTNERSHIP

We can now see God has a pattern of funding His workers through the giving of the saints. This model is practical. It engages the Body of Christ, empowers workers, produces spiritual fruit, and earns the obedient an eternal reward.

Scripture liberates us to safely work in partnership with the family of God. We do not have to be unnecessarily burdened or confused by funding models of the past that lack scriptural support and place too much pressure on the missionary yet fail to engage the Body of Christ. No, we are free to pursue partnerships in Christ, but exactly how do we do this in a modern age? Where do we go from here?

In this section, we want to introduce a modern application of God's ancient ways, supplying a roadmap and necessary tools for the journey. We will cover the need for clarity of vision, how to start developing a strategy, and how to prepare for a season of partnership development. When we understand the core concepts of vision, gathering, sharing, and inviting, then we can develop partnership in any culture, for any ministry, with any level of ministry experience.

CHAPTER EIGHT

A Proven Model for Partnership Development

It's about the process.

In part 2, we discovered the way in which God supplied for His servants in Old and New Testament times. First, He gave a vision or mission to someone. Next, that individual gathered people together to share the vision. Then, God stirred the hearts of those who heard the vision. And, finally, people gave as they were invited to partner in the vision.

In previous chapters, we saw ways in which the funding model appeared to be customized to fit God's purposes. For example, we can recall David's deciding only to gather together his leaders, rather than all the children of Israel, when he chose to communicate his vision. This informs us that there is room for us to tweak how we apply or implement the model. In other words, we can develop a model that is suitable to our times and culture while remaining true to the proven pattern we saw in Scripture for funding missions. And from that proven model for partnership development, we can create a process that applies the model.

What is the proven model for partnership development? It incorporates four elements: 1) receiving a vision, 2) preparing for contact, 3) gathering others, and 4) sharing the vision with them and inviting them to be a part of that vision through giving. Notice the similarity between these elements and those of our biblical model.

To apply the model for partnership, there are certain things we must do or a specific process we must follow. I have found this process to be an efficient and effective way to gather partners. We will take a look at that process near the end of this chapter. Before we do, we need to establish the basis for any action we take in partnership development.

Loving Well

Galatians 5:6 says, "For in Christ Jesus neither circumcision nor uncircumcision avails anything, but faith working through love." Though the subject the apostle Paul addressed was circumcision, we find this beautiful insight that is key, not only for this verse, but for our lives and even our discussion of partnership development. And that key is this: *nothing we do counts if we are not exercising our faith through love.*

When we talk about developing a partnership team, it is important to note that we are not trying to figure out how to make money so we can serve God more easily. We are not trying to do spiritual telethons, product sales, or take offerings through the mail in order to get people to give to our ministry. Those things are fine in and of themselves, and there may be a proper time and place for them. We, however, are learning how to raise a team of people who will link arms with us and join us in walking out our vision.

We are a part of the family of God, and as I have said before, the family business is missions. God wants his family working together, loving and supporting one another. It is our good pleasure to do so. Similar to an athletic team or a symphony, the family of God works in unison, each playing his or her role, to accomplish something together that cannot be done by an individual alone.

Regardless of one's occupation, every born-again believer should desire to walk in right relationship with the Lord and other members of the Body of Christ. We are part of a spiritual family, and this family should not be spiritually dysfunctional but healthy. It is our heartfelt desire to fulfill the great commandment: to love the Lord with all of our heart, mind, soul, and strength. We also want to love our neighbors as ourselves. After all, our love for the Lord compels us to love others well.

We want this to be true with everyone we encounter, including the people we meet in the course of ministry, as well as those we talk to about financial partnership. I am not talking about being nice to people so they will give to our cause. On the contrary, I am talking about loving well because the love of God is in us, genuinely compelling us to love others because He first loved us and commands us to love (see Jn. 15:9–17). We want love to be our motivation. We do not want to treat people as if they are ATMs. When we look at others, we should not see dollar signs. We should not see them merely as contacts, prospects, targets, or leads. They are our brothers and sisters in the Lord, and they should be treated with love, respect, and honor, at all cost—all the time.

Building a financial partnership team is not a numbers game where, if we just get enough names and make enough phone calls, then we will have what we want. No! We are members of a family, kings and priests to our God. We have been redeemed by the blood of the Lamb. Therefore, we need to treat others accordingly.

In developing a partnership team, then, one of our greatest desires is to build healthy relationships that last for eternity. We do not want to lower the bar on love so that we can raise more money. We want to move forward, carrying our assignments and sharing with the Body of Christ. Together, as the family of God, we will accomplish His will.

The kind of relationship I am talking about is possible with a financial partnership team. I personally have great relationships with people on my team. I have not lost any friends by talking about money, but I have gained many more relationships. Actually, the partnership has strengthened my relationships. I have had missionaries share with me how great their team building time has been, too. A missionary friend told me one of his partners said, "Our partnership is the most significant spiritual relationship we have."

See, we don't have to sell, we don't need to market, but we do need to share. We aren't in the business to make money, but we do want to move forward with the family working together.

Remember *propempō*, the Greek word from chapter 5? It means to outfit for the journey, to put gold in the purse and bread in the sack; it means to encourage, to support, to join them on the way, to journey together. We want to walk in *propempō* with the family of God.

The Contact Process

In order for us to be successful in developing a ministry team, we need to start by connecting with the people we know, and we need to do it in a personal, humble, and time-effective way. The best and fastest way to build a team of long-term, deeply committed partners is to talk with them face-to-face and invite them to be a part of our team. Because of the limited time we all have, we want to have an effective system that reaches a large number of people at the deepest heart level. We could do a mass mailing and contact two hundred people in a weekend, but this would be impersonal, ineffective in its communication, and fail to provide the important face-to-face meeting. It would result in very little partnership.

Meeting with people face-to-face is the best way to go in building a long-term team. People respect the fact that we would take the time to talk with them, and the face-to-face interaction gives us a chance to communicate our heart and gives our prospective partner a chance to hear our excitement and vision. Sharing with fellow believers about how God is moving in missions can be very encouraging to the hearer, and it brings glory to God. Face-to-face meetings help build confidence within others that is necessary for them to partner with us as workers trying to obey God.

So if the best way to build a long-term team is through face-to-face meetings with people, then we need to develop a process whereby we can make that happen. Our model instructs us to share the vision with people, but just how do we go about doing that? We do this via a four-step process.

The Four-Step Process of Partnership Development

Our four-step process is not something new. It is not the latest in marketing, and it is not a clever sales approach. Actually, it is a modern-day application of communication with this simple goal: to build a long-term team with whom we will walk in *propempō*.

We want the process that allows us to operate in the confidence and safety of Scripture but, at the same time, reaches the Body of Christ in an effective way so that we can share this very important opportunity for the Great Commission. We want the process that honors the Lord and the people of God, giving them time and room to make an informed decision. This process needs to provide an opportunity for the Holy Spirit to stir people's hearts, and it needs to value the best forms of communication in order to share an important message. A good process will reach the largest number of people at the deepest heart level in a time-effective way. I have found the following process of partnership development to meet our criteria: 1) send a letter, 2) follow up with a postcard, 3) call to ask for an appointment, and 4) have a face-to-face appointment.

Let me give a little explanation. Our goal is to share, not convince or persuade, and our goal isn't even securing the money. We want to get in front of people, share the vision, allow the Holy Spirit to do His work, and then invite them to be a part of the vision. Remember, the model of partnership development needs a process by which it can fulfill its goal. And the goal is to share with a brother or sister in person.

We will go into more detail explaining how to do each step in the following chapters, but for now let me begin to draw a little picture of what this will look like:

1. Send an *invitation* letter (about four or five weeks before you can meet face-to-face).

2. Send a follow-up postcard (about seven days after the letter has been sent out).

3. Make a phone call to ask for an appointment (five to seven days after the postcard has been sent out).

4. Have a face-to-face appointment to share and invite (typically, about four to seven days after the phone conversation).

As we can see, the face-to-face connect is the fourth point of contact. This gives our brother or sister a comfortable time to consider our invitation to missions. The first three points of contact are made without ever leaving the house. With this method in mind, we move through three points of contact before we ever talk face-to-face (see "Illustration 1: Contact Process Chart"). When we do get our face-to-face appointment, it is with someone who could have said *no* at three different points before but has chosen not to. This puts us in face-to-face meetings with the right people.

Often, I have had missionaries share with me the benefits of this model. They have said, "It gives me a starting point and a plan." Some have even said, "It helps remove the cold call feeling."

Occasionally, they share their partner's remarks, like, "Wow, the postcard was helpful. I had forgotten about the letter and to pray." One pastor recently shared, "I've given money to ministries and missionaries for a lot of years, but the experience I had recently with a missionary at ABC ministries [name changed] has been different than any other. This is the first time I've been kindly and graciously pursued in this way. In fact, at one point when I wanted to give this couple my financial support, they wouldn't let me! They wanted to speak to me face-to-face before they would accept anything, and that personal connection made all the difference in the world. I don't just feel like an anonymous donor, but know I truly am a partner in ministry with them!"

Conclusion

God is going to advance His purposes in the earth, and He wants to do it with us as we work together in love and service to one another. We cannot and should not try to fulfill the call of God on our lives alone; we need others to partner with us over the long term. The benefits of developing a team include providing opportunities for the greater Body of Christ—connecting believers with missions, advancing the Great Commission, and strengthening the organization we are serving.

We need to identify the vision God has given us, and we need to learn to communicate it simply. We are servants called into occupational ministry, and when we share, the person needs to hear a servant trying to obey. In other words, most potential partners need to see God at work in a person they are thinking about partnering with and see that the individual is going to bear fruit for the kingdom of God.

Looking Inside

- If you currently partner with a ministry, did you make that decision the first second you heard about the ministry or were given the opportunity to give, or was it a decision made over time?

- Have you ever made a financial commitment over the phone with a telemarketer?

- Do you feel as though a multi-step process is necessary?

- Do you feel that a high level of relational equity is required for partnership? Has this assumption kept you from asking?

Taking Action

1. People partner when they have confidence and trust in the person sharing the vision with them. Start writing down your story about how the Lord has called and led you. It may have started back when you were nine years old and heard a missionary share at church. How did the Lord call you? What were the circumstances, Bible verses, dreams, or events that led to that call? Think it through and write it down. What have been the high-water marks in your walk with the Lord? How did He call you to the ministry? How did you enter your current field of service? This should be no more than a page or two.

2. Start communicating with others on a regular basis. Don't be out of sight and out of mind. Start sending a newsletter; be intentional about outreach to build relationships. Start a blog. Go to parties, weddings, and other social events. Pray for people and then send them a short encouraging email. Make it a goal to reach out and connect with two hundred individuals within the next six months, by face-to-face meetings, emails, texts, Facebook, or phone calls. This amounts to about one reach per day.

CHAPTER NINE

Define Vision

Vision is your ministry assignment from the Lord articulated.

The first step in our model for partnership development is receiving a vision. We receive our ministry assignment or vision as the Lord makes it known to us or as the Lord calls us. Indeed, the will of God or vision for our lives is knowable. It is ascertainable. When the Lord calls people into ministry—making known His will for their lives—no matter the time in history, I believe He does so in one of three ways—through divine calling, divine placement, or deep desire.

But let's talk a moment about the word *calling*. In the New Testament, it is often used to express *the divine call* or *the gospel call* that invites us to salvation. Scripturally speaking, *calling* also refers to the work or ministry one is appointed to. But there are even more ways people use the expression in Christian vernacular—ways even that diminish its true significance.

We usually use the word *calling* to stress something that's important or non-optional to our Christian faith. We will say things like, "I'm called to prayer," or, "The Lord has called me to serve my neighbor," or possibly, "I'm called to serve my family."

These are all common calls in the Christian life. When we look in Scripture, on the other hand, we read about very specific callings to particular individuals. I think of men like Abraham or Moses or Samuel. We can see the real impact the event of the call had on not only the men themselves, but on other people for generations that followed. I mean, men like these heard God's voice directed to them, announcing their mission and providing them with vision for their life's work. In essence, they received a divine summons.

Calling (A Divine Summons)

When a person is called in Scripture, it is a divine sovereign move of the Lord, where He makes a formal request. We could describe it as a divine summons for a person to do the work of God.

For example, Moses was chosen by God to be a deliverer for the people of Israel from Egyptian bondage. For much of his life, he grew up in an Egyptian home. He may have heard the prophecies about the promised deliverer, but there was that moment in time where God began to move in his heart (see Acts 7:23; Heb. 11:24–27). This eventually led him to the desert where he tended sheep for his father-in-law, Jethro (see Ex. 3:2ff). It was there during a routine day of shepherding that the Lord called to him from the burning bush. Moses stopped and turned aside; then the Lord spoke to him and gave him an assignment to be the deliverer of the people of Israel. It seems that Moses' calling began when he was forty, he went through a period of consecration in the desert from age forty to eighty as he shepherded flocks, and then he was commissioned at the burning bush.

Another example of a person being divinely summonsed would be King David. David was a young man, possibly in his teens, when he was shepherding his father's sheep in the countryside. One day the prophet Samuel approached him and said, "Yes, this is the one." Then he proceeded to pour out oil from a horn and prophesy to David about being the king of Israel (see 1 Sam. 16:12–13). David was divinely called. It wasn't something he had stirring in his own heart or something he pursued on his own. I am sure he wasn't watching sheep one night and thought to himself, "Boy, it would be great to be king of Israel one day." It wasn't a dream, it wasn't his idea, and it wasn't a practical decision he made by weighing the pros and cons of the office. David was summoned by the Lord to lead His people.

Another example of someone being called by God would be the apostle Paul in the New Testament. Paul was on a road traveling to Damascus, looking to arrest any followers of Christ, when Jesus Himself showed up in a powerful way and called him to serve Him. Paul was a Jewish man who loved God, but he lacked revelation and understanding about Jesus, his Messiah, and the New Covenant. Paul was actually in the process of persecuting believers when he encountered Jesus on the road. In Acts 9:15, Jesus says that Paul was a chosen vessel to bear His name before the Gentiles. Paul did not have it in his heart to be an apostle, and he was not led into it over a period of time. No, he was converted, suddenly called, and that in dramatic fashion.

In the three examples above, we can see that there is a specific time of calling, a time of consecration, and then a time of commissioning. Moses was called when he was forty, then he went through forty years of consecration, and then he was commissioned to actually deliver Israel when he was eighty years old. Likewise, David was called as a teen, went through seven years of consecration serving Saul and running from him, and then later he was commissioned and actually became king. Paul was called in a day, but then he withdrew and spent time in the desert before he really moved into his apostolic ministry. In much the same way, the twelve disciples were invited to follow Jesus, and then they went through about three years of consecration and preparation before they were later commissioned as apostles to do the work of ministry.

Divine Placement

Another way the Lord brings us into full-time ministry is what I call *divine placement.* I still think of it as a calling even though the Lord works in more of a hidden way to us. He leads us without our being told directly what is going on. It works something like this. We love the Lord and pursue a life of prayer and obedience. We try to sincerely love Jesus the best way we know how, giving ourselves to fellowship and the breaking of bread. In the process, we put one foot in front of the other, and before we know it, the Lord brings us to a place where things become very clear. We look around and discover we are at a place, among a people, and doing ministry when we never planned it or heard a divine call to do it. We have simply obeyed the slightest leadings of the Holy Spirit. Those little nudges are His way of saying, "Over here, come over here." And we simply go toward Him without thinking about where we are going or what He is calling us to.

Back in 1991, I had a dramatic encounter with the Lord, and within a few moments I was born again. Within about twenty-four hours of being born again, the Lord spoke to me about full-time ministry. It wasn't a divine summons; it was more like, "This is what I want you to do, and I want you to pay attention, and I want you to get ready for it," type of call. I had a sense of an assignment from the Lord, but He wasn't "sending" me right away.

So I prepared, served, studied, and prayed, and I grew in my love for Jesus. I had quite an appetite for the Word and gave myself to a lot of reading and studying. I served my church family the best way I knew how and listened to my leaders. It was another fifteen years, however, before the Lord actually "commissioned" me into full-time ministry. When He commissioned me, it wasn't a summons or a direct order; it was more of a subtle invitation that I couldn't say *no* to.

Sometimes a divine placement sneaks up on us, while at other times the Lord speaks a little bit here and there over years as He did with me. The divine placement, then, is a result of day-to-day obedience, whereby we respond to the gentle leading of the Holy Spirit. So there we are at a place we didn't necessarily foresee. We didn't predict the destination, yet we found ourselves at a threshold, transitioning out of the marketplace into full-time ministry, for example. We suddenly realize the situation wasn't one we sought or pursued, but because of our love for Jesus, we obeyed and followed Him.

Sometimes this divine placement can also be in the form of a gentle impression on our spirits. We may have this feeling on the inside where we just know we have to move into ministry. Often, we can't imagine doing anything else. The thought of not responding to full-time ministry puts a major check in our spirits, and we feel as though we would be disobedient if we didn't move ahead in ministry. The calling, then, is not a case of being told, "You do this and go there." No, it's more of being divinely led.

Deep Desire

The third way I see people move into ministry or serve the Lord in some capacity would be what I call a *deep desire*. In this case, the Lord places a desire inside of us for His Word, for loving Him and others, for obeying, and for serving. The desire arises, and we find ourselves wanting to be in full-time ministry. Or maybe we have an inward desire that wants nothing but to serve the Lord in a full-time capacity. We are not responding to a divine summons. Neither are we being divinely placed by Him, but we just have a holy desire on the inside that we choose to act upon. Maybe we express it through a prayer: "I would love to serve orphans in Africa. Would You let me, God?" Sometimes the Lord endorses or gives us permission to do what we ask Him based on our sincere desire alone.

I believe the Lord may grant a request to serve that is made in humility and sincerity. Psalm 37:4 says, "Delight yourself also in the Lord, and He shall give you the desires of your heart." This verse isn't about full-time ministry, but it does show the importance of our first delighting in God and His seeing our holy desire and hearing requests that flow from our hearts.

First Timothy 3:1 says, "This is a faithful saying: If a man desires the position of a bishop, he desires a good work." An overseer is the same as a bishop, elder, ruler, leader, and pastor—all are used interchangeably, describing the same office. There is a lot required of an overseer—much more than desire. But Paul makes it clear this is a position that can be desired or aspired to, and that this desire is a good thing.

Calling Turned into Vision

Our greatest joy as servants of the Lord is in attending to and fulfilling the will of our Master. When we are brought into a place of full-time occupational ministry, be it by divine calling, divine placement, or deep desire, we need to know what our assignment or role is in order to obey it. "What is my life's assignment as it pertains to occupational ministry? How do I need to spend my life in order to hear the Lord say to me when I finished my race, 'Well done, good and faithful servant'?"

When we have clarity on our occupational service assignment and know how we need to spend our lives, we have vision. The vision I am talking about is not a business strategy, a tag line, or even a clever way to market our assignment. The vision I'm speaking of when it comes to partnership development is clarity on the thing that God has given us to do or the deep desire He has placed within us.

Servants need to know what is on the heart of their master in order to know how to serve well. A humble servant doesn't have plans and ambitions of his or her own; the servant's plans are his or her master's plans. Or to say it another way, the master's ambitions are the servant's ambitions.

With that in mind, we need to ask ourselves, "What one thing has the Lord spoken to me? What single phrase did He give in His divine summons? Where has God divinely placed me, and what do I need to do in order to obey what He has put in my heart?" When we answer these questions, our vision becomes clear, and we understand what we must do to serve the Lord. Just for the record, our sense of doing or being shouldn't be out of compulsion or a raw sense of duty; rather, it should be because of love. I want to obey my Master, to fulfill His vision for my life, because I love Him and He loves me.

Typically, believers growing up in a Christian context are not trained on how to hear the voice of God or how to determine the will of God for their lives. Hearing God's voice is often presented in some nebulous or mysterious way. Additionally, they are not taught how to live as a living sacrifice before the Lord. These elements are extremely important for any believer to understand, but they are especially important to the servant who is called to full-time ministry.

The first thing that we have to know is what the Lord is saying to us. Because we were neither trained nor equipped on how to know and understand the will of God, His will can be a mystery to us. Knowing what God has spoken to us and knowing what He has placed before us are extremely important to clarifying our vision. Understanding the assignment God wants us to carry out is knowable. It doesn't have to remain a mystery forever. I personally have learned to hear and understand what the Lord is saying to me. I know what my assignment is, and I'm walking it out. I believe we can learn to hear His voice as He promised His disciples (see Jn. 10:27).

There is a more sure way of knowing that this is true, however. When we consider the fact that the Lord Jesus is a righteous Judge and one day we will stand before Him as He assesses our service to Him, we know His judgment will only be righteous if our assignment was knowable and doable. It would be unfair of Jesus to judge us for an incomplete assignment if that assignment was shrouded in such mystery that there was no way to know His will. Proverbs 25:2 tells us, "It is the glory of God to conceal a matter, but the glory of kings is to search out a matter." We can know God's will for our lives. It may not be plain and obvious at first, but we can search it out through prayer.

Creating Our Vision Statement

If we do not have a vision for our lives, we need to start a dialogue with God and discover what His will is for us. We should take time to ask Him questions and listen to His answers, and record what He says. I have included some questions below to get us started. These questions are designed to place us in the position of servants who are yielded to our Master, ready to do what

He communicates to our hearts. I recommend taking one question at a time and spending a few days or a week praying about that specific question. We shouldn't move on to the next question until we feel like we have received an answer from the Lord.

Here are the four questions to ask the Lord:

1. If money and circumstances were not a problem, how would I serve You, Lord?

2. Jesus, how do You want to spend my life, and what do You want to purchase for Yourself through it?

3. Lord, in terms of my service assignment, what must I do to stand before You without regret?

4. Lord, what are You asking me to do in this current season as Your servant? What must I do to obey Your will for my life?

Each time we ask a question, we need to wait for the Lord to reply. He may drop a phrase into our minds or move on our spirits with a gentle impression. We must pay careful attention here, take notes, and write down the thoughts that come to us. We should consider keeping the question before the Lord for several minutes, maybe twenty or more, and asking it in different ways. Then we want to spend time meditating, listening, and staying tender before Him. It is important to pay attention to the movement of our hearts and the impressions that come to mind, jotting down notes and phrases we think the Lord may be saying, without processing too much or being too analytical. We simply should write down what comes to us.

After working through each question listed above, giving it the proper time of prayer and meditation, it is time to take our notes from our dialogue with Him and start organizing them and writing them into clearer thoughts and statements. The goal is to end up with clear statements about what we feel the Lord is asking us to do. This, of course, will take a little more time of prayer and meditation.

When we write out our notes, it may be a page or less. After we have written down what we feel the Lord is saying to do, then we start condensing it. We wrestle through each concept and really focus on what the Lord is asking of us, weeding out all other thoughts, dreams, or ambitions. It is important to work through these statements until we can state our assignment in one or two short sentences.

Our vision statement should not look like a job description within an organization. It should be a little bigger, a little broader, and a little more general than a job description. For me personally, my one sentence flowed out of Jeremiah 3, where the Lord said He was giving good shepherds to Israel who would feed with knowledge and understanding so that Israel would return to her Bridegroom God. My one sentence was something like this: "I know the Lord has called me to be a good shepherd who feeds with knowledge and understanding so that believers come into the fullness of Christ." I can be a good shepherd on college campuses in the United States, or I can do it as a church planter in Asia. But I can also do it as a teacher at a university in Europe.

There are several ways that my life can give expression to being a good shepherd that feeds with knowledge and understanding, but this one thing I know for sure, that my life has to be about shepherding; it has to be about feeding with knowledge and understanding. If I'm not doing this as a lifestyle, then I know that it's going to lead to regret when I stand before the Lord at His judgment seat. Because I know that I'm called to feed with knowledge and understanding, I also know that I have to be a good student of His Word, I need to have a prayer life that is vibrant, and I actually have to know the Lord. How can I be a good shepherd if I don't know *the* Good Shepherd?

Once we have one sentence written down, then we need to practice saying it in several different ways. We want this vision statement to be a part of us, to be in us, so that we can communicate it clearly to others and know it for ourselves. We should be able to say it conversationally so it doesn't sound like an advertisement slogan or a tag line that we have memorized.

Our Vision Serving Our Future

Getting this one-sentence vision statement will serve us well in the future. Even though it is a hard exercise, it's worth the time we put into it. When we get this vision statement written down, it will give clarity and focus for our lives. It will put strength in our spirits as we move forward to serve the Lord.

This one-sentence vision statement is like the destination goal in the distant horizon. If we are only looking at the ground in front of us, we can often drift off course very easily, but if we raise our heads up, we have that focal point in the distance. This makes it much easier to stay on course so we don't wander to the left or the right.

Understanding our vision will also help us say *no* to many good opportunities that come our way so that we can say yes to the ones actually assigned to us. I'm not talking about disobeying what God has spoken to us. I mean, what often happens in the area of full-time ministry is that we can become surrounded by opportunity and need that is overwhelming. And because of love and compassion, and in a sincere desire to obey, we can find ourselves falling into dozens of different things that pull us off course and draw us away from the original thing that God has called us to do. Having the clarity of vision, setting it on the horizon, and making it our goal can help us wade through the territory that is saturated with need and opportunity.

Having a clear vision statement is important because our model for walking in biblical partnership is driven by vision. The model doesn't work at all if we don't have clarity of assignment from the Lord or if we are not clear on that deep desire He has placed within us. As I said at the opening of this chapter, our process for partnership development includes extending an invitation for people to join us in ministry. Partnership, itself, is an invitation to a shared vision. In partnership development, we are asking people to join us, to link arms with us, to be part of a team that accomplishes something together that could not be done by an individual alone.

When we lack vision, our invitation is going to be confusing at best. The receivers won't hear the clear call to be a part of what we are doing. The other reason that vision is so important in this process of partnership development is because it is challenging. It is labor intensive and takes time and skills. Partnership development can be socially challenging, but it is biblical and can be engaged in with a right heart. Without clarity of vision and conviction of the assignment, we will not press through the difficulties and the rigors of it.

Conclusion

We were designed by God to partner with vision. When we hear it and it resonates inside us, we will be able to serve the purpose of God with spiritual strength and endurance. Vision gives us strength when we are weak. It also gives us purpose and direction, keeping us on course. Vision doesn't have to be grand or sensational, but it does have to be clear. Most likely, God has already put vision in us—and that vision can be discovered, known, and shared.

Looking Inside

- Do you have vision, direction, and goals for your life (i.e., family, education, service, etc.)?

- Does your life lack specific direction, and are you drifting due to a lack of vision?

- Is the stewardship of your life vision-driven? What could you do to improve?

- How could a clear vision currently change your life?

Taking Action

1. Go look up five ministries you are familiar with, either on their websites or their ministry materials. Find their vision statement, and read it carefully two or three times.

2. Analyze the vision statement by asking yourself the following questions:

   - Is the statement full of vision, or is it a description of what they do?

   - Does the statement excite you, or is it just okay?

   - Is the statement new and fresh, or does it sound like a dozen other vision statements?

   - Does the statement stir your heart, pull you higher, and make you want to join the ministry?

   - Does the statement stimulate your imagination and fill you with hope?

   - Is the statement only something God can achieve?

   - Does it preach or quote a Bible verse? (Most times it should not.)

   - Does it contain specific spiritual language associated with the organization? (Hint: It shouldn't.)

   - If achieved, will it glorify God, make His name great, and advance His purposes in the earth?

CHAPTER TEN

Prepare for Contact

You hit homeruns not by chance but by preparation.
—*Roger Maris*[1]

As we launch out into building our financial partnership team, we need to make sure that we are ready. A key to being successful in any partnership development is good planning. The more we plan, strategize, and make real, obtainable goals before we begin, the more successful we will be.

Remember our discussion of David from chapter 4? Once he had permission to work on the temple, he spent a considerable amount of time preparing before he shared with his leaders or started any work. David gathered stone cutters and masons, and he collected so much iron and bronze that it could not be measured. He secured cedar trees and made blueprints, the design of which came from the Holy Spirit. David also wrote down the divisions of the priests, singers, musicians, and other jobs within the temple. Because of his planning and the favor of the Lord, the temple project was a success.

Any journey starts with a destination in mind. When we fail to plan, we plan to fail. In order to effectively prepare for a journey, then, we must know where we are going, plot the best course in order to get there, implement our strategy, and stick to the plan. Jesus had a lot to say about long-term vision, counting the cost, and planning (see Lk. 14:28–32).

In all of my years of training and coaching missionaries in partnership development, preparation is an area where I see consistent mistakes being made. Most underestimate the importance of planning and the length of time needed to do it. This often results in their waiting too long to start their partnership development, potentially creating an unnecessary financial crisis and causing them to launch out under pressure. When we begin this way, we will feel rushed and won't take the proper time to prepare, develop, and practice before we implement. I want to add that I have seen missionaries who have not done due diligence in their preparation, overly relying on their own personalities or spirituality to get them through. Their planning has lacked detail. This, too, is problematic. We need to remind ourselves that the Holy Spirit likes plans and do our part to prepare.

Creating a Contact List

After we have clearly defined our vision, it is important to start putting together a list of people with whom we could share that vision, and as much as it is possible, we are going to share with them face-to-face and one-on-one. There are a number of people we know right now, people we could include in our mission by sharing our vision. Whenever I address this topic, most people begin to draw back or filter out people. They think of their past relationships or how long it has been since they last saw or spoke with these individuals. I try my best to encourage them to not draw back, to not apply that type of filter just yet. At this point in the process, it is necessary to include those names, to add them to the contact list. We need to believe that God has a team for us and that many want to hear about what He is doing through our ministry.

We ought to take the time to sit down and write out all the names of the people we know—friends, family, and acquaintances. The only criteria for our name list is that we know an individual's name and he or she knows ours. If that is the case, then we write it down. This list isn't necessarily a mailing list that we are going to send information to, but right now we are only brainstorming people we know or have met. We want to get this list as large as we can. For most people, even those who think they do not know many people, this list typically builds to include over two hundred people! Honestly, we know many more people than we think.

When we take the time to create our list, we will begin to see we have many potential people who we can sit down with and share the vision God has given us. Writing out this list of names is not a trivial thing to do. We simply cannot rely on our memory to have names at immediate recall. So we need to take the time— preferably an hour or two a day—working on our list. But if we don't have that kind of time each day, then ten minutes over the course of several days will suffice. The first 60 or 70 percent of our list will come very quickly, but the last 30 or 40 percent will come harder for us and, consequently, take some more time. We may have to push ourselves a little, but it will be worth it in the end.

While coaching missionaries in partnership development, many of them have submitted lists of only sixty or seventy names. Typically, I remind them of different "people" categories like associations, churches, clubs, or small groups. This usually pricks their memories, causing them to recall more names of individuals to include on their lists. They return a few days later with a hundred or so names. I mention a few more people groups and send them off to continue working on their name lists. They return a few days later with even more names. I have seen this cycle continue for days, and a name list that started at sixty-five ends up at two hundred and twenty. I specifically remember one young woman who started with twenty-eight names, but once I got her to stop filtering the list and move past her comfort zone, she ended up with three hundred more names. She is currently serving in full-time ministry, funded.

To help get us started, here are some practical suggestions on how to go about making a list:

- Find a comfortable seat, sit down, and write out all the names of the people you know. A good place to start is with your closest friends and family, your immediate contacts.

- To prod your mind for more names, think about different people groups—other friends or more distant relatives, friends of your friends, family of your family, neighbors, etc. They are a great place to begin the brainstorming process.

- Next, think about those who go to your church. You could even start by looking through the church directory, if your church has one, and writing down the names of the people you see on Sunday. These could be the people you attend home group with, or the people with whom you have worked at church. Go through a mental list of everybody you have been in church with and begin to write the names down as they come to you. For many of us, that could be more than two hundred people alone!

• Still in need of names? Use "Illustration 2: Contact Idea List" to find other categories of people to help you brainstorm and remember other people you know. Even consider some of the places you have worked or coworkers you had in the past. Write their names down as well.

The idea behind brainstorming for names of people we know is to start thinking through every area of our lives—who we went to church with, where we have worked, where we went to school, what different clubs and associations we have been a part of. We should even consider the people we typically encounter every day, individuals we know at the bank, grocery store, dentist, doctor, or school. All of these are people we have contact with, individuals we can talk to about our vision.

Let's not forget social media. We can look through our Facebook friends and our email accounts, and several more names will come to mind. We may look at an old school yearbook and find the names and faces of people we went to school with or were roommates with and write down their names, even if we don't have contact information for them right now.

Once we have worked on this for several days and we are down to the point where we are only adding maybe one name every three of four days, then we are really close to our list being done. After that, we move to the next step: gathering contact information.

Gathering Contact Information

Gathering contact information is probably the most challenging part of this process. We can come up with two hundred to five hundred names, but then finding addresses, phone numbers, and other contact information can be challenging. It takes both a lot of work and a lot of time to do this. I recommend that we spend several minutes a day trying to search out and find this contact information. Although gathering is the most time-consuming and slowest part of this process, we can do it.

Even though this is a challenging part of the process, it is vitally important in order to be able to sit down with them and share the vision that God has given us. Let me give some practical ways that I have found helpful to gather contact information. Some people's information is public knowledge, and if we go through Google's white pages, we can then submit a list of names. If their information is public knowledge, their contact information will show up on Google pages. This doesn't work with every contact in every situation, but a number of people on our list will appear, helping us gather their mailing addresses or phone numbers.

It can also be helpful to gather information from a church directory. We want to be sure to use a church directory ethically, however. If our home church has such a directory, we can feel free to use it. We may be well connected with a church, and upon request, it offers us its directory. We don't use a directory where we have almost no connection or relationship. Directories are mostly for in-house use. We need to respect that. Facebook and other social media sites are another effective way to gather contact information, and I typically start with a personal message to each individual. I will say something to the effect of, "Jim, Rob Parker here. I would like to stay connected with you and keep you up to date on what's going on in my life and ministry. Here is my contact information. May I have yours?" I then wait patiently for a reply. We can't make people reply, but if they do, it is important to keep a dialogue going.

In the event that my subtle reach fails, I just make a direct appeal for their contact information. When I have a phone number, I will call and ask for the person's mailing address. In some situations, depending on how well I know the individual, I will text and ask for his or her mailing address and other contact information. When I don't have a number or email address, and the soft approach isn't working, I will write a personal message on Facebook. It may read something like this: "I would like to have your contact information so I can stay in touch with you and share with you about my ministry. May I have your phone number, mailing address, and email?" With simple requests such as these, a number of people will share their information with us.

Another way to gather contact information is through a mutual friend. Sometimes one of my friends has a better relationship than I do with the person I'm trying to contact, so I will ask my friend for the other person's contact information. Sometimes I will run into people at church and ask them for their information.

Lastly, our parents' address books and Christmas card lists are other places to gather information. We can be creative while gathering contacts.

Organizing Our Contacts

Once we are close to gathering most of our contact information, it is time to move on to organizing our name list. It is a subjective exercise that pays off in the end. We organize our list into three separate groups: groups A, B, and C. I organize these groups based on what I understand my level of relationship to be with a specific person. I put all my best relationships in group A, which are those people with whom I have the closest fellowship—the people I can talk to anytime, anywhere. These are the people with whom I often have coffee or lunch, and I can easily hang out with them for an hour or two at a time and talk about almost anything.

Group B contains people I know fairly well, but they are a bit more like acquaintances than close friends. These are the people with whom, if I ran into them at the store, I could easily talk for five or ten minutes without it being awkward. However, they are people I may never share a meal with or meet for coffee on a monthly basis. A lot of people at church fall into this category. I see them and know their names, I can easily talk to them for a few minutes, but we don't do much together outside of church.

Then my C group has in it any individuals who did not fit into group A or B. This is a good category to put those relationships I have had in the past but maybe I have not spoken to them in many years. This could include people whom I have met a few times, but they are really friends of friends. We don't need to worry about sharing with someone we haven't talked to in years. People don't need as much relational equity as we think they do.

As believers, our motivation for giving into the Great Commission is altogether different than giving in any other financial situation. I know of a missionary who approached a former classmate he barely knew and hadn't spoken to in over twenty years. Upon sharing God's vision and ministry, the classmate shared a ten-thousand-dollar gift with his ministry. And this is simply one of many stories I could tell where individuals we would not expect to partner with us actually become a true part of our team.

Mapping Out a Campaign

Just a quick note about the word *campaign*. I am using this word to mean a season of heightened focus on partnership development. It is much like individuals running for political office. Candidates spend a season meeting people, talking, sharing, and inviting them to show their support. A partnership campaign is a focused season of meeting, sharing, and inviting. This may require that we travel to several different cites, regions, or possibly countries.

After our contacts are organized into groups, it is time to begin to map out a campaign. Making room for a campaign is hard for those who are already in full-time ministry because it means much of the ministry has to slow down or completely stop for a time. Most people don't feel they can step away from the mission of God they are engaged in for a time to focus on raising funds, but this step must not be skipped.

One of the advantages of giving ourselves to partnership development and focusing on it in a very real way for an extended period of time is that we will develop a measure of momentum that makes it easier and more productive. Giving proper time to develop partners is one of the greatest investments we can make for the long-term fruitfulness of our ministry.

Another advantage of an extended campaign is that it creates momentum when we are in a specific area for a period of time. When people hear that we are in a geographical location for a period of time, we have a better chance at being able to meet together, seeing we have made ourselves available to them over a number of days. This, then, creates more opportunities to meet with more people. The extended time makes room for meeting with new people as well. When missionaries come home on furlough, they should be prepared to take three to six months to focus as much as possible on partnership development.

I have seen a number of single people take a three-month season to completely focus on partnership development. They work forty or more hours a week on it, raising a substantial amount of financial partnership in just ninety days. I have seen married couples spend five or six months building the proper partnership team needed to serve unhindered, too. No matter our age or whether or not we have a family, focusing solely on partnership development is essential to fulfilling the call of God on our lives.

Only we can determine for ourselves how much time we need to focus on this, but I recommend that we work at it until we have achieved our financial goal. We should fight for the opportunity to be properly funded *before* we start our ministry assignment. When we are engaged in ministry while trying to raise support, it becomes much more difficult because of the added pressures that ministry brings. There are so many demands and needs for ministry that it is really hard to shut that down and give our partnership development the proper time that is necessary. As difficult as it may be to find the time in the midst of ministry, we have to find that time. We should consider taking short trips, maybe a week or two, to connect with people, focusing on partnership development. We can also consider travel to a nearby city for a weekend, or even weaving in partnership meetings as we travel. We have to look ahead and give it proper planning. Remember, when we go, we want to meet them face-to-face and share the vision God has given us.

Spring and fall are ideal times to begin. The peak of summer, at least in the United States, can create challenges with vacationing families while the kids are on summer break. Summer is not impossible, but it will be a little harder to schedule appointments. Many people go back to school even as early as mid-August, and so I have found March through June is a great time to be campaigning.

For a fall campaign, we start sending our letters in August, and then we do the appointments in September, October, and most of November. By mid to late November, we have to shut the campaign down while wrapping up appointments. Thanksgiving through Christmas and on into the New Year is a difficult time to effectively schedule appointments, since it is a busy time of the year for most people. Although, it is a great time to reconnect, visit with people, and build relationships.

I recommend launching our campaigns in the spring and in the fall, then. Here is a simple action plan on doing this:

1. Map out the cities you can go to where you will have the most impact and be able to connect with the greatest number of people.

2. Map out the dates you plan to be there, remembering that the more you plan, the more detailed your strategy is, the more successful you will be in the long run.

3. Document the cities you want to visit, estimate your arrival and departure dates, and the dates that you will use for follow-up and transition from one region to another.

4. Create a list of people you want to meet and share with in each area, and be sure to list the potential churches you want to visit and share with too, as well as small groups and Bible studies.

Develop Our Materials

Once we have this campaign mapped out, then it is time to start developing our materials. A few materials are absolutely necessary to reach out and to raise partnership, conduct appointments, and solidify that partnership. One of the materials we might want to develop is a letterhead so the letters we send out look more professional. If we are in a situation where the mission agency we are working with doesn't provide one, then we can create our own with a ministry title and some contact information where potential partners can contact us.

We can also develop postcards, a bifold or trifold, or a little ministry booklet that gives more information about what we are doing, the call of God on our lives, and an invitation for people to partner with what God is doing through our ministry. If the organization we are with doesn't have all the material that is needed, we may have to play a part in helping develop it. Any ministry materials we can share in the form of hardcopy would be great.

Additionally, we will need materials for the appointment itself. As we conduct partnership meetings, we want to have everything that we need to share in the appointment, to extend an invitation to partnership, and then to wrap up the details of that partnership. Therefore, we need to develop a partnership commitment card as well as give instructions on how people can partner with us.

It is necessary to develop all the materials that are needed before we start campaigning. We don't want to be developing our postcard while our letter is already in the mail, and we don't want to be developing ministry materials on the way to an appointment. We must take the time, think it through, create a list of materials we want to develop, do our research, and then put the time in to do the work. We should get these materials developed and in our hands before we start our campaign.

Practice, Practice, Practice

The next thing that we would do before we launch out is practice, practice, practice. We might have had twenty-five thousand phone calls in our lifetime, but we have not had this one particular phone call before, and maybe we have done lots of one-on-one meetings but probably not in the area of partnership development. Our ministry in the Great Commission is of primary importance; therefore, we want to be prepared and properly funded. Again, let's practice before we go.

A missionary who had gone through my partnership training course said, "Preparing for a season of development is a lot of work. I spent hours and hours writing, designing, planning, and practicing. Every hour I spent preparing was effort; learning new habits and new skills isn't easy. At times it was frustrating. But once I started my one-on-one appointments, I was able to share with clarity and confidence. I knew what to say, how to respond to questions, and best practices for the approach and follow-up. At times the amount of meetings I was having, calls I was making, notes I was taking should have been overwhelming. But because I had practiced and prepared, I was able to walk out that season with skill and strength."

When we are stressed out, our brains do not process as well. We get confused and forget things, and our communication is often not as clear as it could be. The more comfortable we get through practice, the clearer we will think in our meetings. Even our speech will slow down, we won't be as nervous, we will articulate better, and we will have more fun. In short, we will be more confident, and this confidence will be imparted to the person with whom we are meeting, which will be important in their partnership decision.

A marathon runner spends months, and possibly even years, preparing for one race. His training, his diet, and his coaching all help him prepare. He puts in a tremendous amount of work before he ever steps into that race. In the same way, we want to set out and determine the call of God on our lives, gather the tools necessary, and develop the proper skills to fulfill that call. The tools not only need to be gathered, but we must get them sharp, practice with them, and then launch out.

Conclusion

We are going to look at some more tools as we continue on in the next two chapters, but I cannot stress enough the need for strategic planning. Failure to plan here will cause us to be more likely to fail down the road, never hitting our target or reaching our goals. When we take the time to plan out our method for partnership development, we will be more likely to hit our target.

God has called us, we have a job to do, and we want to be faithful servants to His call. Without developing a team of people who will stand with us in prayer and financial partnership, it will be much harder, if not nearly impossible, to do. God not only has called us, but He has called people to gather around us and help us fulfill His purposes in the earth. Therefore, we must do all we can to prepare to meet with the people God is calling to run alongside us.

Looking Inside

- What major achievement in your life did not require preparation, practice, and planning?

- What are the top five obstacles that potentially stand in the way of your vision being fulfilled (it could be lack of training, finances, ailments, debt, biblical understanding, pride, fear, lack of motivation, lack of skill, etc.)?

Taking Action

1. Look at the top five obstacles from the above list and write them down.

2. Take obstacle number one and sit down for about thirty to forty minutes praying, asking God for wisdom and a plan to overcome that obstacle. Write down at least five things (action steps) you have to do to overcome the obstacle. Take the next obstacle and do the same. Repeat until you have worked your way through the list. Write it down and keep it in a safe place (see "Illustration 3: Vision, Obstacles, Goals").

CHAPTER ELEVEN

Gather People

Decision-making is a process; lead people through the process.

Making a first impression is important, especially when it comes to developing partners. For many of those we will interact with throughout our campaign, our invitation letter and post-card will be the first time they hear about the call of God on our lives. We are going to look at the need to be both professional and personal in our letter; we will discuss the various sections of the invitation letter we send out; we will learn how to write and design our postcard; and we will review some dynamics of a phone call. The aim of this chapter is to help us introduce our story and our call to ministry, followed by an invitation for others to be a part of it. Let's look at the three points of contact leading up to our face-to-face meeting.

First Point of Contact: The Letter

For many of the people we know, this will be the first letter they receive from us. This is our chance to make a good first impression. With our letter, we will want to be sure to communicate the right message with clarity and concision.

This letter is only the first point of contact we are going to have with an individual, and it should be viewed as leading up to our face-to-face appointment with this particular person. Because of this, our letter is not the place to tell our entire story and life vision in detail. If we want anyone to actually read our letter from beginning to end, then we need to make sure to keep it short and on point.

Our letter is primarily an invitation to pray about financial partnership and to talk further. We are *not* going to do the formal request for partnership here, but we are going to inform our prospective partners about the call of God on our lives and *then* invite them to be a part of it. It is simply an invitation for them to pray about being a part of our team through their prayers and financial partnership. The full and more formal invitation will be done at the face-to-face meeting.

The typical missions "ask letter" usually says something like this: "If you would like to support me, here's how you can: send your faith gift to 123 ABC Street, Holy Town, U.S.A." In contrast to this, our letter is asking others to pray about financial partnership and to let them know that we will follow up in the future and talk further. But even though we are sharing the vision that God has put in our hearts, there are a few things to remember as we make our letter.

BE PERSONAL AND PROFESSIONAL

Most people will only spend a few seconds scanning a letter before deciding whether or not they are going to read it. The first thing they will scan is the P.S. and then the headline. Therefore, we want to make our headline somewhat catchy and also write our P.S. by hand. We want to make our P.S. a personal and a concise summary of the whole letter.

Next, readers will scan headlines, pictures, and anything that catches their eye before deciding to read the rest of the letter. Therefore, the letter must be well written, concise, clear, and grab their attention. We may want to include a picture of ourselves and also include all of our contact information. We may even want to send a brochure or information about our ministry or organization (if it's brief) because this will help them grasp what we do without having to take up more space in the letter.

Though we don't have to hire someone to design our letter, we do need to make sure the layout is easy on the eye. So we will need to make good use of white space, using no less than one-inch margins. And we should use a comfortable font size, at least eleven-point font, leaving some room on the bottom for our handwritten P.S.

It really helps to write our letter with one person in mind as it gives the letter a more personal feel. So we want to avoid saying things like, "Dear family and friends," but instead say, "Dear John and Jane." We don't want to write, "I hope to visit with all of you," but choose to personalize the communication by writing, "I hope to visit with *you*." In other words, we need to write to one person and not to a crowd. We want our friends and family to feel the personal nature of this important invitation.

If we want, it may be good to write a couple different versions of our letter, depending on who is receiving it. We could write one for family, another for nonfamily, another for close friends, one for not-so-close friends, and still another for conservative believers. The different versions of the letter should be 95 percent the same, tweaking it here and there as needed to fit our readers.

In our letter, as well as any other written or verbal communication that we make, we do not want to be presumptuous. Neither should we use manipulative language. For example, we don't want to say, "I will be calling you in a few days to *set* an appointment." Instead, we should say, "I will be calling you in a few days, and I *hope* to have an opportunity to share more with you about the ministry God has called me to."

It is important to remember that this is only an invitation, and that means those we are contacting could decline it. We should not assume that we already have an appointment, or that they are going to partner with us. We are going to honor them, show respect, allow them to pray, and be thankful when they give us their time. There is no need for the hard sell or the use of dramatic language in developing a partnership team. We are on an assignment from the Lord, and He has given us a vision to walk out in love and integrity.

FORMAT OF THE LETTER

We should try our best to keep the headline to a short sentence. The headline should communicate the move to full-time ministry, or at least the basic nature of our ministry. Naturally, the reader's eyes will go to the headline before reading the letter, so we need to get his or her attention here. We don't need to be over the top or sensational, but clear. When we print our letter, we can make this headline bold and large, using a different font style than that of the body text.

Section one is for bringing our friends up to date on what has been taking place in our lives. We share concisely what we have been doing over the last three months. This section is a conversation starter and gives the reader a sense of what our lives currently look like, helping them connect to what has been taking place. If we have been in ministry for some time, we can adjust our language accordingly. It is good to share the work or training we have been doing as well as some fruit from our labors. We can include a testimony here, and we must be sure to express our excitement.

Section two is for describing how the Lord has worked in our lives. This may be an occupational change or new directive we have received, and this is our chance to inform our prospective partners how God led us to this shift in life direction. If we have already been in ministry for some time, we can recast vision and share about the season we are currently in and where the Lord is taking us.

If our readers are assured that we are following the leading of God, it will help them to be more confident in partnering with us. They need to know that the decision we are making to be in full-time ministry is one of obedience to God—not merely our trying out something new because it sounds fun. People will be encouraged that we are responding in obedience to the Lord's leadership.

Even though we may be writing to a friend, it is still important we make the right impression about our occupational decision as well as our approach and attitude toward ministry. In short, we share how God has led us to this decision and state the ministry assignment He has put into our hearts.

Section three will have two parts contained in it: the vision and values of our organization, and our current role within it. We can start this section with either of the two parts, but in general it works best most of the time to lead with the vision and values of the organization. We share their vision, the "why we exist," what they are doing, with whom, and the goal of the projects they are engaged in. We also share the important values, the three things we want everyone to know about our organization. Using language our organization has developed will help here as we keep the message consistent and correctly represent the organization.

Then we summarize what it is that we will be doing within that organization. This is a chance for us to paint a mini-picture of what our ministry work will look like in general. We want to give them a visual impression as best we can, so I would recommend not just making a bullet point list. If we are in a supporting role, we need to be sure to show how important this supportive role is to our department and the organization we work for. If we have a brochure, we may mention in this paragraph that we are enclosing it for them.

Section four is for explaining missionary support, partnership, and giving the invitation. Remember, they need to hear that we are responding to God's leading, and that this is a full-time ministry or a full-time occupational change for us. To rightly express this, we should use an excited tone, mention financial partnership, and ask them to pray about possibly partnering with us.

HANDWRITTEN NOTE

After we have finished our letter, we need to include that handwritten message for the P.S. We will address it to the individuals personally, revealing our excitement and that we look forward to the chance of sharing more with them. The handwritten P.S. will help make the letter more personal and a little less formal. This is also the place where we will share with them that we will be contacting them soon, which will help them move toward prayer, thus beginning the decision-making process.

Second Point of Contact: The Postcard

A point of contact does not have to be flashy; it just needs to be a point of contact. A postcard is a great way to connect with people. They are easy to create, they are fairly inexpensive, and they are very effective in communicating with the potential partner. If the organization we work with has a postcard, then we should use it. But if they don't, then we can make our own if we would like. All we need is just a little creativity, a printer, and some card stock.

If we don't want to make our own from scratch, there are several online services that have templates and will even help us create and print them. We can upload our pictures and graphics and write our text, and in about seven working days, we have our postcards at our doorstep. We can also have postcards printed at a UPS store, FedEx Office, Staples, postcards.com, Vistaprint, etc. If we take time to make a nice postcard, we want to be sure to include our contact information, a picture, and maybe a tag line that captures attention.

Another option for us is to write a short message on a regular greeting card, which can be sent in an envelope, but it will cost a little more than a postcard. We can send a postcard with a postcard stamp that can be bought at our local post office, which is about 40 percent cheaper than a regular stamp. Regardless of which method we choose, our message needs to be handwritten and personalized.

There are those who think they can skip the postcard in order to save some money. But skipping this step will not save us a few dollars in the long run; in fact, it will end up costing us much more money because we will lose contact with potential partners. Everyone needs multiple touch points in order to move through the decision-making process.

At this point, our potential partners will have already received our letter, so there is no need to tell our story again. The postcard is serving as a reminder and providing them with an important second point of contact. We ended our letter by saying that we would contact them soon, and this is our next contact with them. We should borrow from the fourth paragraph of our letter and/or our P.S. to make the text of our postcard.

It is so important that we are following up with them, just as we said we would. We are reminding them to pray about partnering with us, though we don't have to explicitly say it in the postcard. Their hearing from us again will remind them to pray for us and remind them about partnering with us. They should feel our excitement about this new venture God is leading us into, and we are again letting them know we are excited to talk to them soon. The postcard should be sent about seven days after sending our letter. We need to be aware of the mail service and holidays during this time. We would like our friends to have had their letter in hand for about six or seven days when they get our postcard, which is enough time for them to start praying, talking about it with a spouse, and considering our invitation. But we should not wait any longer than seven days to send out the postcard. It all needs to stay fresh in their minds, and we want to follow through on what we said we would do. Any excitement we spark in them can die down if our contact points are spread out too far. There is a good chance that they will not have read our letter yet or have not shared it with their spouses. This postcard will serve as a good reminder for them to do that.

In a digital world, taking the time to write a letter and a postcard can have a real impact and make a good impression. A missionary from Asia shared with me the following story: "I sent a letter to a friend I had not talked to in ten years—not since being born again. My letter was followed by a postcard. I traveled to Asia, and upon arriving called my old friend. He was excited to hear from me, and we set up an appointment. At the appointment, we spent several minutes catching up, but at one point I made the transition to talking about ministry. When I did, he went to his office desk and pulled out my letter and postcard. He was excited to hear about the ministry. I shared with him my ministry and invited him to be a financial partner. I was surprised when he said yes, because it had been more than ten years since we had last talked. He was not even a follower of Christ.

"After our meeting, I decided to ask why he had chosen to partner with me. He said he had always had a heart to share with good causes, but he never had a good connection with the people asking; they just called and asked for money. Sometimes he gave a gift but lacked the confidence needed to be a real partner. He said that my letter, postcard, phone call, and the face-to-face meeting gave him real confidence in me and my ministry. He said, 'I now know that you will do all that you say.' He has been a monthly partner for several years now, and shared many special gifts toward mission trips."

Third Point of Contact: The Phone Call

Before making our calls, we must give ourselves plenty of time to prepare for them. I recommend making several mock calls with friends in the days leading up to our first real call. It would be wise to use our outline until the calls become natural and have our friends present us with different true-to-life scenarios to better prepare us for the possible responses we may get while talking to potential partners.

Knowing in advance the approximate date when we will make our first call is good for preparation. This should be about two weeks after our letter was sent out. We need to mark this date on the calendar, pray, and then prepare for it. After we have prepared for this call, there are a couple things to remember when it comes to actually making the call.

- Do not hesitate when it's time to make the phone call. The first call is always the hardest one to make. The fear of the first one is far worse than the experience of the call itself. After the first call, each one gets really easy and really fun.

- Have your phone outline, contact call sheet, and contact information in front of you, along with your appointment book and a pen.

- Also, when you sit down to make your calls, find a quiet place where there will be no distractions. Furthermore, if you are using a cell phone, make sure there is no background noise and there is a good signal. Don't make calls from a coffee shop or from your car. Find a quiet corner of the house or an office. You may have to leave your house or apartment, but you will need a good writing surface with zero distractions.

- Have a way to organize your calls, too. When you are making several calls in a row, it is easy to forget whom you are calling. It's a terrible feeling, while the phone is ringing on the other end, to realize that you don't know the person you just dialed. You *never* want the person on the other end to say, "You just called me five minutes ago!" To help with this, create a call sheet for each set of letters and postcards you send out. For example, the fifteen letters you sent out in group one would have their own call sheet with only those fifteen names and numbers written on it (see "Illustration 4: Call Sheet").

As I have said before and will continue to say, the most effective way to build our partnership is through face-to-face meetings. The phone call is to ask for a face-to-face meeting with that person and to set a date for that meeting to take place. While making our calls, remember *why* we want that face-to-face appointment. It is the most effective way to give us an opportunity to become better acquainted, to share our excitement about our ministry, to build friendship, to provide people with an on-ramp to our ministry through partnership, and to develop our prayer team.

PHONE OUTLINE

When we get ready to make our calls, it will be important to know what we want to say as well as what we don't want to say. In all of our communication with prospective partners, we need to be able to speak clearly and concisely—and our phone conversation should be no different.

It is easy to go into too much detail about our ministry when we are nervous, but instead of doing that, we should focus on setting the appointment with the person. We must stick to this plan, not getting caught up in the details of what we want to ask at the face-to-face meeting. The last thing we want to do after we have sent a well-written letter and a personal postcard is to stumble around on the phone, lacking direction and failing to set an appointment. This is our first chance to really speak to our prospective partner, so we want to be clear and informative. We want to make a good impression.

Let's look specifically at the outline of the phone call itself:

- **Greeting.** Let them know who you are and confirm that you have the individuals you actually want to talk to on the other end. It may be helpful to ask if it is a good time to talk, and if not, try to find out a time that may work better for them. Set a time to call back if need be. But be proactive

here, never leaving it open-ended. And never apologize
for calling.

- **Small talk.** Make sure you only make small talk for just
  a few minutes. Review the person and your relationship
  before you call. Have a conversation point ready; make
  small talk if you have the chance and if it feels natural.
  There is nothing worse than forced small talk. In the midst
  of small talk, keep your ears open and be sensitive to the
  Holy Spirit. Most importantly, be a friend. The last thing a
  person wants is to feel like you are only trying to use them
  to achieve your ends.

- **Say why you are calling.** Transition to asking them to set
  up an appointment where you can meet with them. If they
  didn't have time to read your letter yet, make an appointment to call back in four or five days so they have time to
  read it first. If they ask you to go ahead and share about
  your ministry, encourage them to read the letter and pray
  first. Set a time to call back; do not leave it open-ended. Be
  sure to set a time to call. If they did read the letter, then
  continue on, sharing your excitement about going into
  full-time ministry. They should be hearing excitement
  throughout the whole process: by letter, postcard, text,
  phone call, and appointment. Ask for an opportunity to
  talk and share more with them. If they say *yes*, express
  your appreciation and set a time, date, and location where
  you could meet. Should they say *no*, assure them that they
  have no financial obligation, but that you are excited about
  what the Lord is doing, what He has called you to, and that
  you would like to have an opportunity to share more with
  them. In the event the answer is still *no*, you can ask them

to consider being prayer partners, and also ask them for permission to share your newsletter with them.

- **Set an appointment.** If needed, let them know how long it will take (no more than one hour, unless their only availability is for a weekday lunch, then only thirty or forty minutes). Be flexible, do what works for them, and be creative if you have to. Have your appointment book ready, and be prepared to meet anywhere and anytime they can. Make it easy for them. When they suggest dinner or a time and place, follow their lead as much as possible. When they aren't offering anything, make a few suggestions. Be sure to confirm the time, date, and location, remembering to speak it back to them. Then wrap up the phone call, thank them for the opportunity to share, and mention how much you are looking forward to seeing them.

Overall, we want to keep our calls short to honor our friends' time. Remember, we are going to be calling several people each day. There are times, however, when we might sense a call needs more time to build the relationship, so we should take the time to do it. In some calls, we may find ourselves with an opportunity to offer pastoral care and prayer. When this happens, we want to be faithful to take as much time as they need. We should remain sensitive to their needs and the leading of the Holy Spirit (see "Illustration 6: Phone Call Outline").

Conclusion

In order to develop a partnership team that will link arms with us for the long term, it is important to have at least three different points of contact with prospective partners before the actual face-to-face meeting takes place. The first point of contact we will have with our potential partners is our letter—so we need to make a good first impression. We should communicate our message with clarity and passion, and keep it brief, sharing what is only essential with the understanding that we can share much more at a face-to-face meeting.

After sending out a handwritten postcard as a second point of contact, expressing our excitement about what God is doing in our lives and our desire for them to partner with us, it is time to make the phone call. Once we are in a quiet place with limited distractions, we can call our prospective partners. Again, the goal of the call is not to share all the information that we have about God's call on our lives, but to set up a face-to-face appointment with them, for that is the greatest tool for partnership development, and the subject of our next chapter.

Looking Inside

- Have you ever responded with a significant gift to a mass mailing of a ministry you had very little knowledge of or relationship with?

- Have you ever received electronic newsletters that you never opened, or opened but didn't really read?

- Have you ever been asked to RSVP in a digital communication and you didn't bother to?

- On the rare occasion that you have received a handwritten personal invitation, either a letter or postcard, how did you feel when you first saw it or opened it up?

Taking Action

1. Referring to "Illustration 5: Letter Template," write the first draft of your letter following the guidelines in this chapter. Give yourself a one-hour window where you can write as much as you can in one sitting. Write the first draft by hand. If you don't finish in an hour, give yourself another hour at a different time until finished. Be sure your letter can answer the following questions:

   - Did you capture your reader's attention?

   - Have they been brought up to date on your life?

   - Did you communicate your ministry vision and transition to full-time, vocational ministry?

   - Have you shared a little about the organization and where you will serve?

   - Have you invited them to partner with your ministry through prayer and financial partnership?

2. Once the draft is done, leave it alone for two days, read this chapter again, and then write your second draft. Share your second draft with a couple of friends, and get their feedback. What you're looking for in the feedback is if your letter is clear and the readers know what your calling is and what you are asking them to do.

3. Go online and search for postcard sites. Look for places that allow you to build your own custom postcard. Postcards.com, Vistaprint, The UPS Store, and print shops are good places to start. Start designing a postcard. Remember that less is more.

4. Write out a mock phone conversation following the outline in this chapter. (You may also want to refer to

"Illustration 7: Phone Call Flowchart".) Ask your prospective partners for an appointment. They will say yes. Then walk through setting up a time and location. End the conversation reiterating the time and location details.

CHAPTER TWELVE

Share the Vision & Invite to Partner

It's not about selling; it's about sharing.

The appointment is our opportunity to share what God is doing in us and through our organization while meeting face-to-face with a potential partner. There are a number of things we need to learn in order to be well prepared, build relationships, communicate clearly, and invite people into missions.

In this chapter, we are going to discuss what actually goes into an appointment kit, some basic things to remember about our appointment, and the necessity of having an appointment outline. By being equipped with the information contained in this chapter, we should have a greater confidence for meeting new people, sharing about our organization, and inviting people to play an active role in the Great Commission.

After having successfully sent out our letter and our postcard, and having talked to the potential partner on the phone to set up a face-to-face appointment, what do we need to do next to get ready for the appointment? How do we prepare? Like all the steps before this one, it is vital that we practice for our appointments with friends or family and, if we can, record our practice. Watching a video of ourselves will help us learn from our mistakes.

Mistakes will be made, that is for sure, but it is better to make them while practicing with a friend than with our first five or six potential partners. While practicing with friends, they need to throw three or four different situations at us: specifically, the good appointment, the rough appointment, and the lots-of-questions appointment. They can change the endings of the appointments, too. They could pretend to be people wanting to support us, those who don't want to support us, those who can only commit to pray for us, those who want to give a special gift only, and so on. But again, we must practice, practice, practice when it comes to the appointment.

Pre-Appointment Materials

I have made a couple of references to having an appointment kit while attending our appointments. What goes in our appointment kit? This kit would include a partnership response card, which should include contact information, the giving amount (and frequency), a budget sheet with monthly needs, a short list of both long-term and short-term needs, giving instructions, any material about our ministry we want to share, a self-addressed stamped envelope, a pen, and thank-you cards. All of this can be kept in a nice padded folder or binder.

Before we go to our appointment, we must be fully prepared, and that means dressing appropriately. I don't mean we have to wear a suit to meet with each person. But if we are going to meet a businessperson over a lunch, cut-off shorts and flip-flops are not the best choice of attire. Neither should we overdress, but we want to look neat, well-groomed, and prepared so as to communicate the right message to our potential partners.

Remembering the reason for our appointment will help us tremendously here: we are going to share with someone what the Lord is doing with us and through our organization, and we are going to extend to that individual an invitation to be a part of it. Therefore, we have to stay focused and make the invitation plain and simple. We don't want anyone walking away, wondering what we were asking of him or her. From our information sharing, he or she should have a good understanding of what we are asking.

Many of our appointments are going to be with friends, and we should expect longer meetings of about one and a half or two hours to be fairly standard with this group of people. On several occasions, however, a shorter meeting will be required; therefore, we must be prepared and organized to get our message across, inviting the person to partner with us in about thirty to forty minutes. The more we practice our appointments, the better we will get at sharing our vision and extending an invitation to others to participate.

In the event that we use a computer, iPad, or a flipbook presentation, we want to have all of this together in a neat package that is ready to go at all times. We should ensure all devices are properly charged, so as to avoid using power cords, and any videos are queued up. It is important to organize our material in a way where we know where everything is. The last thing we want is to be searching for materials minutes before an appointment, and we don't want to be in the middle of an appointment and discover that we forgot to bring something. This would not make a good impression.

Again, we need to think through our presentation and know what we want to say. This is the moment we have been working toward; we now have our face-to-face meeting and a chance to share the exciting ministry God has called us into. The persons we are sitting across the table from have had many chances to say *no*, but they haven't yet. That should encourage us. We asked for an opportunity to share with them, and they said yes. We have prepared for this, we know our vision, we know our calling, and we have confidence that God has brought us to this point—He is going to provide for us. Before we go, we want to pray and ask the Lord for clarity.

The thought of this appointment might make us nervous, but it always goes much better than we think. I remember a young missionary telling me about her first appointment. She said, "When it came time to do my first appointment, I was terrified. I didn't know what to expect. As I sat in the coffee shop, I moved around in my chair trying to find a comfortable position but found no relief. I fidgeted and rustled right up until my potential partner came through the door.

"At this point I really started to sweat. When we finally got back to our table and sat down, she shared with me, 'My day was terrible and so hard. The only thing that kept me going through the day was knowing that I would see you at the end of it. Tell me, what are you doing?'

"At this point I knew that my time with her was going to be about ministry and serving the Body of Christ—and I can do that. From there out, the nervousness with the appointments was gone; I was simply on a mission to serve Jesus by serving others."

We can use our letter as an outline for our conversation, as this is our opportunity to unpack all that wasn't said in that letter. We can spend three to nine minutes or more on each one of our letter's paragraphs. Using our letter as an outline instead of trying to memorize a presentation is not only helpful, but it causes the interaction to be more conversational and natural.

We have to be ready to answer questions the potential partners may ask, keeping our answers short to help them and us stay on track. Good eye contact is a must. And remember, we need to be confident and try not to ramble. Let's throw off nervousness because people are much more ready to give than we think, and besides, they are happy to see us.

When they say *yes*, that is the best time to tell them thank you. We also want to find out what their frequency and level of partnership is going to be. So we ask them questions like, "How much would you like to give? How often would you like to do so?" It is also a good time to have them fill out the partnership commitment card that we brought along in our kit, providing them with our giving instructions, too. We need to have a copy that we can leave with them. We can thank our new partners again and then share fellowship with them.

Outline of Our Appointment

It is my desire to offer tangible, concrete, real-life examples that we can implement in our appointments. I want to give a general outline of how our appointments may look. Again, this is only a basic guide. It can be adjusted or improvised upon as needed.

We can begin our appointment by a greeting and small talk—asking our friends about their family, interests, hobbies, and heart for missions. These are all good talking points. We may share some old memories or talk about old friends we have in common. While we ask a couple of questions about different areas of their lives, we must listen well, taking mental notes as they talk. If we have an hour or longer appointment, then ten minutes of small talk is plenty, but no more than that. If we are having dinner with a friend, then all of the dinnertime could be small talk. We do want to move toward sharing our vision after we eat. If we are meeting with a person we have little relationship with, then we will take time to build rapport with them.

Next, we need to eventually transition from the small talk to something more significant. We can start our transition by saying, "John and Jane, thank you for meeting me here and giving me a chance to share with you about how the Lord has called me into ministry and how He is impacting young adults at XYZ University." Then we proceed to update them about what is going on in our lives. We may tell them where we have been and what we have been doing. We are simply catching them up on what has happened in our lives since the last time we talked or at least from the last three months of our ministry. This would be a great time to share a recent testimony with them.

We will want to share about how we were called into full-time ministry, relating when and how the Lord started speaking to us about this calling, how it developed, and how we first responded. Then we can bring this part of the story up to the present and be sure to share how the Lord has led us to this point.

After relating how God has called us, we will share the vision God has given us. This is one of the areas where being confident is most important. Our confidence will give them confidence. Again, let's be natural while sharing the vision, but we must show our excitement at the same time. We need to show them we are excited about our vision because, if we don't, then they probably won't get excited about it either. If God has truly given us a vision, then I am sure we will be excited. So let's communicate this with conviction and clarity—but also with a sincere heart.

After sharing our vision, we will want to share about the missions organization that we are working for, conveying the overall vision of our missions organization—what it does and where the organization does it. We can mention unique things about our mission. If we are sharing a short video, we may want to start it at this point. If this is the case, we may mention here that our missions organization requires all missionaries to raise their own support, so we need to be ready to answer any questions as to why that is.

It is also good to make room for questions throughout this process. If people are being asked to give time and resources to something, they are going to have questions about it. Again, this is a conversation that is to be taking place more than it is our making some presentation. We could even ask them at points throughout, "Do you have any questions?" We want to make sure the air is clear before we invite them to partner with us.

After answering any questions they may have, it is time to invite them to partner with us in ministry. Many people at this point lose confidence and begin to apologize for needing to raise support. But if we are convinced from the Scriptures that we are doing this God's way, then we should be confident about asking them to partner with us. We will need to pause shortly, and then transition with a restating of our vision/call in one sentence. We do not want to "hem and haw" around, look away or down as if we are embarrassed. We should look those we are speaking to straight in the eye and say, "John and Jane, will you partner with me in ministry?"

Once we have said this, we will be tempted to look away or say something because we may be uncomfortable with the silent pause. Again, we should remember why we are doing this and simply continue to look them in the eye and wait for the answer. I might mention that we are not staring them down, though. We simply wait and allow them to be the next ones to talk. Once they do, we respond accordingly (see "Illustration 8: Appointment Outline").

If they say *no*—and it is always a real possibility—try to discern the *no*. If it is a clear no, then we move toward asking them to consider being a prayer partner or giving a special gift. If they say yes, then we have them fill out a commitment card with how much they would like to give.

By the time of the appointment, most people know the dollar amount of their partnership. If they say, "Well, what would help you?" Then we can say, "I want you to feel like a part of our team, so I encourage you to partner in a way that excites your heart." If they express a desire to partner with us but are not sure about monthly partnership, we should listen closely and try to help them weigh what they could do. We want to be ready to make a way for the quarterly, yearly, or occasional giver. If they seem to have decided how they would like to partner, then we move toward wrapping up the conversation.

If the no is not clear, if they hesitate with something like, "Well, I uh, I don't know," then we can ask questions to gain clarity and be ready to give explanation for whatever questions they may have in return. If they are still not sure, then we can ask them to partner with us through prayer. Here again, we thank them and move toward wrapping up the conversation.

When they say *yes*, we thank them for partnering with us. At this point, it is good to find out the amount they would like to give and how often they would like to give it. Once those details are worked out, we can complete filling out the partnership card with them and go over the instructions for giving.

With all of this completed, we close the appointment, thanking them for taking the time to meet with us and then maybe extending an invitation to be a prayer partner. We hand them a partnership card and give pertinent instructions on how they can pray. It is important to spend some time fellowshipping with them at this point. If we are there for true partnership, we don't make them feel as if we were just there to get something from them and give them a presentation. No matter if they choose to partner with us or not, they need to feel loved and cared for. The closing of the appointment is a perfect time to show that to them.

As soon as we leave the appointment, we send them a thank-you card. In it, we talk about our time together and how much we look forward to partnering with them in the future. It is good to mention the dollar amount they partnered for and comment on how much it will help. We need to let them know what their partnership will accomplish: outreach, salvations, training, intercession, mission trips, acts of justice, mercy deeds, etc.

Fear of the appointment is a far worse experience than the appointment itself. My experience has shown me people are pleasantly surprised by the number of others who are excited and encouraged to hear from them. They didn't have to give us an appointment, but they did. With the missionaries we have trained, while in appointments, we have seen tears of joy, and amazing times of fellowship. It is wonderful to see people encouraged about missions and many willing to be involved. We have seen incredible acts of generosity, including people buying computers, paying for airline tickets, covering tuition, giving five-digit gifts, committing to be four-digit monthly partners, paying for houses, buying cars, paying off student loans, and lots of prayer and encouragement. I know it may be surprising, but actually, this whole process can be fun and enjoyable for all parties involved.

A Key Component of Our Partnership Team: Excited Friends

People who say *yes* to partnership (both financial and prayer) are the ones most excited about our ministry. And these individuals often have friends who possibly could be interested in learning about our mission. I refer to these friends of friends as *excited friends*. Excited friends are key to building our complete partnership team. When we do our partnership campaign the way we have described in this book, 30 percent or more of our team will be people we currently do not know. It will be difficult for us to reach our fully funded mark—as well as stay properly funded—apart from excited friends.

Connecting with people outside our own circles is key to long-term success in ministry, and it is good for the Body of Christ as a whole. Many would be happy to be a part of our ministry; they just don't know we exist. Friends we already have relationship with are a great way to meet more excited, like-minded people.

Excited friends are not referrals, leads, contacts, or warm prospects, but brothers and sisters in Christ who share in our interests and concerns surrounding the Great Commission. They want to see Jesus' name lifted high and His fame go throughout the earth. These are people who would be happy to sow into us and our organization; they only need a chance to meet us and hear our story.

The best time to talk about excited friends is during our face-to-face appointments. Once we have talked about partnership, have had them fill out a partnership card, and have shared the giving instructions, then we want to address the topic of excited friends. I will also ask about excited friends when I receive a *no* to the partnership invitation if the person is happy for me and excited about my ministry.

Some people want to use excited friends as "plan B" in the event that they don't meet their financial goal with their closest friends. I would advise us not to make this mistake. In the appointment, our excitement is high, and momentum and interest are being generated. Trying to revisit the topic later on, however, is much more challenging. The best time to talk about excited friends is in the first face-to-face meeting.

When we are asking to meet their excited friends, we have to choose our words carefully, in a way that our friends can hear our heart behind the request we are making. If we sound like we are only hunting for contacts, our friends may disconnect and shut down before we have a chance to be heard. So we must remain focused on the mission at hand.

As we work through our outline, here are a few things that I want people to hear as I share and ask. I want them to hear gratitude, and I want them to hear the opportunity for their involvement. I also want them to clearly hear my situation, that people are stirred and joining my team. Most of all, I want them to clearly hear what I am asking them to do. Here are some steps with specific dialogue on how to ask them about excited friends.

STEP ONE: ACKNOWLEDGE AND INFORM

"Jim and Jane, *thank you so much for your willingness* to be a financial partner with me in the work at ABC Ministries. *There is another vital way that you can be a part* of this financial partnership team."

If they said *no* to partnership but are happy for us and excited by the ministry, then we inform them that there is another way they can be involved.

STEP TWO: DESCRIBE OUR SITUATION

"In this season I am working on building a ministry team of financial partners who will work with me in reaching teens for Christ through ABC Ministries. God has given me several opportunities to share about how He is moving through this exciting ministry and impacting teens with the gospel. As we have been meeting with friends, they have introduced us to their friends, and many have been stirred by God to become financial partners with us in ministry. Currently, I have not yet met all the people needed to complete our team."

In the language above, they:

- hear my situation.

- hear that friends are introducing me to their friends.

- hear that friends and friends of friends are stirred and becoming partners.

STEP THREE: ASK FOR AN INTRODUCTION

As I have said, confidence is a key to being successful in developing financial partnership. We must have confidence in our calling, that God is able and that He has a team for us.

"Jim and Jane, while I'm here in Omaha for the next two weeks, I plan to meet as many people as I can, sharing with them about how God is changing the lives of teenagers through ABC, informing them about ways they could be involved. Will you introduce me to your friends, by letter, email, or phone, so they can have a chance to hear how God is moving through this ministry?"

The language above clearly communicates:

- I plan to share with as many people as I can.

- I want them to have a chance to hear about the ministry.

- I am asking them to introduce me to their friends.

We must be very clear in what we want people to do for us. When we use the right language and ask correctly, they will usually say *yes* to introducing us to their friends. If we are hearing noes in our appointments, then we should talk with our coach, allowing him or her to instruct us on how to ask correctly. A young missionary friend I work with learned how to ask correctly. In a three-month campaign, she gathered the names of over four hundred excited friends.

STEP FOUR: WHO ARE THE PEOPLE?

Maintaining a confident attitude, we ask who the people are in their lives who would be excited by this ministry or share in their concern for whatever our ministry focus is. We should ask the question in the positive, "Who are the people in your church?" We don't want to ask this passively, like, "You don't happen to know anybody, do ya?" or "Do you know anybody who might wanna give to our ministry?" We need to use action-oriented words and buzz-words for our organization that represent the ministry:

- "Impacting college students through the love of Christ."

- "Planting churches in Southeast Asia."

- "Taking the love and truth of Jesus Christ to the nations."

- "Who shares in our concern for the fatherless?"

The persons we are talking to have two to three hundred of their own friends at church and work, and in social settings and their family. We help them think of names by breaking down their lives into smaller categories. With pen in hand and our copy of "Illustration 10: The Excited Friends Flowchart," we ask for names: "Jim, who are the people at your church who share in your excitement for planting churches in Asia?"

As they share, we write the names down on our flowchart. We can try to get two or three names before moving on, asking basically the same question again in a different context, with a different set of action words and buzzwords: "Jim, how about your men's ministry? Who are the people there that share in your concern for reaching the lost?"

Again, we try to get a few names before moving on to the next context: "Jim, how about your work? Who are the people there that share in your excitement for taking the gospel to unreached regions?"

Different contexts to ask about people could include home church, Bible study, men's or women's ministry, home group, workplace, neighbors, family, and social settings like hobby clubs or recreation groups.

It is good to keep the persons we are meeting with *thinking*. We want to work through the groups of their friends one at a time. We need to avoid suggesting more than one at a time.

After compiling a list of names, we ask them for help in prioritizing our list. We can say something like this: "If you were in my situation, raising a financial partnership team so that you could fully obey the Lord with XYZ Ministries, who on this list would you talk to first?"

STEP FIVE: WHO IS DOING THE CONTACTING?

Now that we have gathered a number of names, we need to find out who is going to do the contacting. We want to honor all existing relationships, not stress them. We can assume that they would like to do the contacting and mention it first in our question. For example: "Jim, will you contact them, or do you think I should?" If they would like to do the contacting, then offer them a prewritten letter of recommendation or a prewritten email. If they are calling their friend, we ask them when we can make the follow-up call. Or we may ask if they would possibly introduce us to their friend in person.

Then we want to encourage them to make that contact. A call would be great, and their communication should be something like this: "I would like you to have a chance to meet my friend, Chris. He is in full-time ministry at XYZ. I think you would enjoy his ministry as much as I have. Can Chris have permission to contact you? Would that be okay with you?" Then we listen for the excited friend's response. (Note: Our partner may want to send a little communication in writing to their friend before we call, or we may want to do that ourselves, depending on who is doing the contacting.)

STEP SIX: GATHER CONTACT INFORMATION IF NEEDED

If our friends or new partners have decided to do the contacting, then we don't need contact information yet. That can come in a few days, once our friends have contacted their excited friend. In the situation where we are doing the contacting, now is the time to gather that information and gather as much as our friend has. The contact information we have may determine the method of contact.

STEP SEVEN: FOLLOW THROUGH

If we make the call first, we follow our standard outline. We identify ourselves and help them know who we are: "Hello, Mr. Smith. My name is Sally Singer—we have a mutual friend, Mike Jones. I think he shared with you that I would be calling." Then we take a minute to build rapport, perhaps even around our mutual friend: "Well, Mr. Smith, the reason that I am calling is that I was recently talking with our friend, Mike Jones. I was sharing with him about the work that the Lord is doing through our ministry at XYZ. Mr. Smith, have you heard about XYZ?"

We respond accordingly, ready to give a one-minute overview, if necessary—"XYZ is an evangelical . . ." Then we ask for an opportunity to share, where we set appointment details. Later we can consider sending a brief letter with a ministry overview, or written materials about the ministry, and/or possibly a video link. It is advisable to send something with a photo and contact information.

Finally, we will go to the appointment. We may differ in the ways we invite others to partner. We just need to be sensitive to the Lord's leading. We have two options here: we can invite directly by saying, "Will you partner with me in ministry?" Or we can invite them indirectly by saying, "Will you pray and ask God what part He might have you play in this ministry?" Then we follow up with them in a few days. The fact is, we will need to follow up with a large percentage of excited friends after the appointment, no matter what we do.

Conclusion

Face-to-face meetings are the best way to develop partners who will commit to prayer and giving financially for the long term. Everything we have been doing has led up to this point where we get to sit down with potential partners, tell them about our call to full-time ministry and what we are trying to do, and then invite them to share in the work that God is doing. It will be surprising to see how God powerfully works on our behalf.

Most people who say *yes* to partnership or are excited about the ministry are happy to recommend us and the ministry to their friends. Over 30 percent of our overall team will be made up of excited friends, which means it will be difficult to reach our properly funded goal without them. They aren't referrals, leads, or contacts. They are brothers and sisters in Christ who share similar concerns about the Great Commission. More than anything else, having confidence in the Lord's willingness to provide a partnership team for us will enable us to ask clear questions that aren't weak but action-oriented.

Looking Inside

- Do you enjoy giving to missions? Would you love to hear about how God is moving in missions? Would you gladly support the ministry of a friend in missions? Do you think you're the only person who feels this way?

- Are you excited by the opportunity to share how God is moving through your ministry? Can you share God's story and invite others to be a part of it?

- Do you believe that right now, this very minute, there are people who would love to sow into your ministry but haven't met you yet?

- Do you believe that God has a team for you, that He wants to give you new friends?

- Do you believe that God wants to see you successfully complete your ministry assignment, even more than you do?

Taking Action

- You have just entered an appointment in someone's home or in a public place. You have little or no relationship with this person. Greet him or her warmly and help set the tone of your meeting. Be prepared to carry the first couple of minutes of the greeting time by yourself. Write out at least one page of your greeting conversation.

- Write out a good outline for an appointment, following the suggestions in this chapter. Make it a two-layer outline with one or two sentences at each point (see "Illustration 9: Appointment Flowchart").

- Make an appointment outline and stick to it. Your appointment invitation has ended with a *yes* or a very positive, excited *no*. Now you want to ask about excited friends. Pick the conversation up with, "Mr. Smith, there is another way you could help with our ministry." Write one to two pages. Practice both your appointments, asking for excited friends with friends and coworkers. Record the practice with video and learn from your mistakes. Practice it as much as you need to until you are comfortable. This may mean you have to do it twenty-five or thirty times[1] (see "Illustration 10: Excited Friends Flowchart").

PART FOUR:
EXPANDING & KEEPING OUR TEAM

In order to develop a team of ministry partners who will enable us to fulfill the call of God with faithfulness, it will take more than meeting with a few friends and family members. Missions is our lifestyle and along with it is developing ministry partnerships. We are working in relationship with the family of God and, therefore, want to love everyone we meet and love them well.

In this section, we will cover additional strategies for meeting and sharing with new people that are simple, fun, and very effective. This will include hosting small groups and approaching churches for support. Additionally, I want to share a few ideas about how to stay connected with our team through newsletters and face-to-face visits. Lastly, I want to provide a few stories from missionaries just like us, who have been successful at building their partnership teams and are faithfully serving the Lord in their ministry assignments.

CHAPTER THIRTEEN

Extend Our Reach

*Multiple strategies in various environments are required
for success.*

Building a solid partnership team that will empower us to
serve God in full-time ministry will require that we implement
more than one strategy during our campaign. I recommend multiple strategies in order to reach the largest group of people on a
personal level in a time-sensitive way.

Our purpose for this chapter will be to cover additional ways
we can develop partnership, how to create a plan for multiple locations, and how to implement the varied strategies in each location.
We should gain the knowledge and skills necessary for a diversi-
fied strategy in our partnership development campaign.

Strategies for Partnership Development

As we develop a strategic plan for our partnership development, it must include both diligence and faith. Planning will take
time and a lot of hard work. We must trust God because He has
called us to ministry and has a team already prepared for us. We

will need to use a combination of the following strategies to raise our partnership team in a way that honors God and helps cultivate partnership for the long term.

One method done by itself does not guarantee success. Furthermore, we must have a strategy for each location that we are engaged in, whether that be individuals in face-to-face appointments, excited friends, cookouts and/or dessert gatherings (hosted by small groups), and churches. We probably have one to three or more areas where most of our contacts are located. We will want to think through which strategies we may want to implement. Sometimes we can implement all four strategies in each location, while at other times we are only able to implement one strategy in each location. As always, we plan well, work hard, and maximize our time.

We can begin by dividing our contacts list (remember, group A, group B, and group C) into groups based on geography. Each city or region should have its own list. Each city or region can be divided into further groups of ten to fifteen contacts. We need to spend some time thinking about how long we need to stay in one area to walk out our partnership strategy with all our contacts, making sure to give ourselves the time we need. We should make that time a priority and fight to protect it.

Most strategies will work best when we are at one location for an extended period of time. In the Chicago area, for example, if we have forty-five contacts, we could separate these into three groups of fifteen. To avoid a bottleneck effect, I rarely send more than fifteen letters per week. I have found fifteen letters to be the max number, any more than that, and it becomes difficult to complete them in a week. Then the following week, I have a new group of fifteen plus last week's leftovers. The longer we go the worse it gets. Additionally, we will be calling excited friends, hosts for small groups, and churches, and making follow up calls. Fifteen is the largest number of letters we can send and keep up with all the other commitments. Because of the amount of contacts we have in Chicago, we would be there no less than three weeks—that's one week for each group of fifteen. Additionally, one to two days a week should be designated for follow-up and transition. Therefore, we would need to be in the city for about three and a half weeks.

Once we plan all of this out, we determine which strategy we will use in each situation. We may use all of them in the same season, in the same city, or on the same trip. We evaluate potential locations like our hometown and, if applicable, our spouse's hometown. We can go to where our parents live, where our friends and relatives are located, or even to cities we have worked in. There is always the possibility to go where good friends/partners have moved to, or even to cities we have ministered in. In the last few chapters, we have been discussing one-on-one meetings as well as excited friends. Here, we will cover two additional strategies: hosted small groups and connecting with churches.

Hosted Small Groups

Hosted small groups, cookouts, or dessert gatherings are all great ways to meet new friends as well. This is similar to asking for and meeting with excited friends, except instead of being

introduced to one person, our current partners or friends would
introduce us to several people at once at a fun and comfortable
small gathering. When done correctly and consistently, this
strategy can considerably strengthen our partnership team.

I have a number of missionary friends who have taken a week,
traveled to another city, and worked through one hosted small
group. It had a two-hundred- to six-hundred-dollar-a-month
impact on their budget. One friend of mine took a week off from
his ministry and traveled to Connecticut where a friend hosted a
small group in his home. My missionary friend met seventeen new
people and followed up with many of them over the next few days.
By the end of the week, he had eleven new partners and thirteen
hundred dollars a month in new support. None of the eleven new
partners had ever met him or heard of his ministry organization
prior to that week.

If we are interested in being hosted in a small group, we can
approach partners or friends about six or seven weeks in advance;
we should ask them if they would host a cookout or dessert social
for us and invite a few of their friends. The first thing we could
do is write a personal recommendation letter. I mean, we write
the letter for our partners or friends. They are the speakers in the
letter, but we take all the work out of it by writing it for them (see
"Illustration 11: Letter/Invitation for Hosted Small Group"). They
would send it to five, six, or seven households about three weeks
prior to the event, which would provide the first point of contact.
Once the invitation arrives and is in their homes for three to five
days, our partners make a phone call, invite the potential excited
friends to come, and confirm the attendance of their friends.

The third time we have contact with these friends of our friends is during the actual gathering. It is here that we will meet and greet our prospective partners, learn a little about their personal history with the Lord, and enjoy the event. When all the guests arrive, our partners will gather the people into their home or meeting place, where we will come to meet them with no presentation or "big ask." Our job is just to meet them, share, and inform them about what God has been doing in our lives.

Once our hosts introduce us, we will share about twenty minutes, maybe thirty if things are going well. We want to keep our sharing conversational, however, as no one wants to be invited to a cookout to hear a lecture. The hosts can ask questions and initiate discussion if things seem a little slow. Once that part of it is done, the hosts can invite the group to interact and mingle. This is our opportunity to move among the guests, ask questions, and learn a lot more about them, having them talk *twice as much* as we do. We can share a *little* about ourselves, but at this point, they will have already heard a lot about us. It is also good to have ministry materials available that our hosts can send home with them.

After the meeting we and the hosts can determine who will follow up and contact the guests, because it will be vital to follow up with them. The hosts can call twenty-four to forty-eight hours later to see if we can contact the guests, or the hosts can send an email asking or informing the guests that they would like to share their guest contact information unless that guest objects, which is the fourth point of contact. Once we receive that information, then we call the guests and ask for an appointment (the fifth point of contact).

The sixth contact takes place when we meet with the guests and ask them to partner with us. Then we can complete any follow-up if needed, sending them newsletters, for example. For our friends who are helping us, there will be a lot of steps involved in this process, so we need to coach them through the letter and through the call. This shouldn't be a problem if we do extensive planning on the front end. Again, we want to do as much of the work as we can for our hosts, making it as easy for them as possible. It should be our desire to provide them with an experience that would make them want to do this again.

Churches

When addressing a church, many of the concepts are the same as approaching an individual but vary slightly because we will likely be speaking to a small group—like a missions committee or elder board. The missions committee probably won't bring us before the entire board to share our vision. Therefore, we will need to give them more information on the front end than we would an individual. They will need enough material to make a decision, assuming they will probably make that decision in one meeting. Therefore, we want to ensure our packet has everything they need to make an informed decision.

THE ESSENTIAL COMPONENTS OF A CHURCH PACKET

The contents of a church packet consist of three primary parts: a cover letter, modified invitation "ask" letter, and a spiritual résumé. All three should be printed on nice paper. We may also add material about the ministry organization (e.g., bifold or trifold brochure, short booklet, etc.) to our packet. Let's look at the individual items in our packets.

The Cover Letter

Our cover letter doesn't need to be long; it is serving only to greet our readers and explain the packet they are holding in their hands. I would suggest creating a header for this cover letter, a simple colored design. Additionally, our cover should include a ministry logo. As we are creating this document, we want it to be both professional and personable in appearance and tone.

The total length of our cover letter should be two short paragraphs, with no more than two to three sentences per paragraph. We begin the letter with a greeting for the specific pastor, missions board, eldership, or church that we are addressing. It is best if this cover letter is addressed specifically to the group of people who make decisions related to missions giving. But if we don't know what that group is, I suggest addressing the cover to either the missions board or the church name.

Modified Invitation Letter

I suggest we use the invitation letter that we have already created and are using for face-to-face appointments. We need to leave our headline at the top of the letter and be sure to include a nice, high quality photo of ourselves. However, we will also have to make changes to the opening and closing paragraphs of this letter. In the first section of our invitation letter, we typically bring people up to speed about our lives over the past three to six months. But because this church packet and the modified invitation letter are going to churches we have little or no relationship with, we need to talk about ourselves a little more. We should introduce ourselves, our occupation, and the organization with which we work.

Likewise, in the fourth section, our invitation will be sensitive to their time, relationship, method of operation, and budget restraints. Churches typically need more time to discuss the opportunity at hand than do individuals. They have many more factors to consider compared to a normal household. Therefore, our invitation will be clear and direct but a little less pinpointed on the time element.

Spiritual Résumé

Because we are looking to develop long-term partnership with churches we may not have a relationship with, a spiritual résumé provides an opportunity for them to get to know us and our history of serving. Our résumé should communicate past ministry experience and training that are pertinent to our occupation in ministry.

Our spiritual résumé doesn't have to be long or done in great detail, but it does need some specific information that is pertinent to those looking at it. It needs to be well done, professional, and clear. It is suggested that 50 percent of pastors applying for a position are rejected based on their résumé presentation alone—because it is sloppy and lacks details. If we need help coming up with a résumé, there are many online resources and templates available. Adding an organizational logo and name on our documents connects us to a ministry that is already established and helps give credibility to us and what we are doing.

Some things we may include in our spiritual résumé are our contact information, mailing address, phone number, email address, and website information. It may be good to include our vision statement and some of our experience, which should be primarily ministry-related but doesn't have to have full-time ministry positions. It can include places we have served within the local church, missions trips we have taken, outreaches we have served on, or other things we have done in ministry.

Next, we will want to include the education that we have, both spiritual and secular, both accredited and non-accredited. This should be an abbreviated bullet point list of the education we received and the year. These don't need any explanation as long as the words we use are descriptive enough. We don't want to list conferences we have attended, unless they were lengthy intensives where we received specialized training. It is best if these are listed from the oldest to the most recent.

Lastly, we will want to include the names and contacts of two or three pastors, leaders, and lay people who know us well.

OTHER THINGS TO CONSIDER

Once we have our packet component parts together, we need to be mindful of some other things like packaging, our selection of churches to contact, the delivery of the packet, and so on.

Packaging

When our church packet is finalized, we can put it into a large envelope with a clasp (with the church personally addressed on the outside), a clear presentation portfolio, or something similar. Whatever we choose to put it in, we should maintain the pattern of being professional and personable. Something that will give this church packet a personal touch is to include one of our postcards with a handwritten note on the back. We simply attach the postcard with a paperclip to the cover letter, positioning it in the middle or lower third of the cover letter.

Selection of Churches

In chapter 10, we had a name brainstorming assignment where we thought of people who we know and then put them into groups based on our relationship with them and the region in which they live. We will want to create a similar list for churches.

We start by doing an Internet search using Google Maps of the churches in our area/region. Google Maps is extremely helpful in giving us church names, street addresses, office hours, websites, street views of the actual church, and phone numbers. When we have a website, we log onto it and find out as much information as we can about the potential church. We watch for contact people to whom we can address our packet. The person may be listed under titles such as Missions Board, Missions Committee, Missions Pastor, or Missions Director. We will want to document this information for future use.

As in our previous assignment, we group churches together in A, B, and C groups. Group A would include churches we have relationship with, churches where close friends and family attend, or churches within our particular denomination. The B group would include evangelical churches, churches that have a missional history, or churches we have limited relationship with. Group C would include all other churches. Churches most likely to partner with us are churches that have two hundred members or more.

This doesn't mean that we should exclude smaller churches. No, however, we can avoid spending too much of our time with smaller ones because small churches often don't have the resource to support ministries outside their own.

Delivery

Many churches are closed on Mondays, and that is often the pastor's day off. So we won't plan to visit a church on Mondays. Likewise, Wednesdays can be really busy too, so we will be sensitive to the church's schedule, which can typically be found on its website. Church offices tend to get busier throughout the day as well, so earlier in the day may be the best time to drop off the packet. As always, we try to deliver it while continuing to be sensitive.

Working with churches tends to be a slower process than working with individuals. The decision oftentimes isn't something they can make right away. Typically, churches have to look at their yearly budget, factor in other giving responsibilities, and timing. They may say yes to partnership and be extremely excited about what we are doing, but they can't start for another six months. On the other hand, we may show up at the right time, and the partnership can begin quickly.

Speaking with a Church Receptionist or Church Contact Person

When we approach the receptionist or contact person, we want to be sure to greet him or her, sharing both our name and asking for his or hers. Being sensitive to his or her time, we may take a minute or two to share about ourselves and what we are doing there.

When speaking to the receptionist, it is important to find out to whom we need to direct the packet and try to get that individual's contact information. Oftentimes, the senior pastor is not the person who makes missions decisions, so we will let the receptionist help us here by possibly making a connection for us.

It would be great to keep this conversation to about three to five minutes. First impressions are lasting, so we don't want to take up all of his or her time. We want to be kind and gracious to this person. We want to give him or her a reason to like us. We want the receptionist working for us, making sure we are heard. Additionally, he or she will be communicating the impression we made to whoever our contact is.

After we leave our church packet with the receptionist, we follow up in person around ten days later. This ten-day time period will probably be enough time for the contact to review our packet, but it isn't long enough for us to fade from memory. If we are no longer in the same city, then we send a postcard as a way to follow up and keep our name on the radar.

When we return to follow up, we should express our gratitude for the person who helped us in the process of connecting with the proper people. So it would be wise to take another couple of minutes to build a little more rapport with that person. I recommend having a prewritten card ready, much like a postcard, to leave for that individual.

Last Thought

Working with churches is similar to working with individuals, in that they need multiple points of contact, they need to hear vision, and they need to see our faces. With most churches, we will need to be faithful with our follow up as well.

When approaching a church, it is important to have a servant's heart. It's God's desire that His family works together in fulfilling the Great Commission. We always look to strengthen, build up, and encourage the local church. We want to help it do things in missions it might never have an opportunity to do on its own. Building partnerships with churches takes time, but it will normally bear fruit in the long run, so we just need to be diligent.

When we get an appointment, we already know what to do. We know to be prepared, be prompt, have an appointment kit and materials ready, be friendly, make good eye contact, engage the board or others in conversation, and share and invite. Following our meeting, we send out our thank-you letter within twenty-four hours. In this situation, I do not recommend sending a postcard. We should send a short, professional letter, which could include something personal about the committee that we learned from our appointment as well as commend them for their heart for missions. A one- or two-paragraph thank-you would be appropriate. And we want to remember to include our handwritten signature.

Conclusion

No one method will ensure that we reach our properly funded mark, which means we may have to use multiple strategies to accomplish our goal. The four primary strategies that we see producing the greatest fruit in partnership are face-to-face appointments, excited friends, hosted small groups, and meeting with churches. Most people have more than one location in which they are developing partnerships, and this means a person will have to create a strategy for each location. Over 75 percent of our budget will come from individuals, so having a close friend or current partner host a small group is an effective way to meet new friends and potential partners. Over 30 percent of our partnership team will be made up of excited friends, so learning how to ask clearly and with a heart to connect these others with their missions interests is key.

Let's not forget churches. They are great potential partners in our ministry assignment, but they will need specific information, time, and a personal approach in order to make an informed decision.

Looking Inside

- Do you have friends or acquaintances living in a city or region other than where you live?

- How many cities or regions can you list, where at least three friends or acquaintances of yours live?

- You could probably name four or five people who would host a small group for you. Who are they?

- How many churches do you have some sort of connection with?

- Look at your list of over two hundred names. Most of them are attending church. How many churches are represented in that list?

Taking Action

- Take one hour to do a little research. List three or more cities or regions you have lived in. Find those cities or regions on Google Maps. Do a search of churches within a fifty-mile radius of these areas, and document all the churches there. Be sure to include all the information you can get from Google Maps as well as the churches' websites.

CHAPTER FOURTEEN

Strengthen Our Team through Yearly Visits

You cannot build good and lasting relationships without occasional face-to-face fellowship.

Meeting face-to-face with our partners once a year is vital to maintaining long-term partnership. We may be in the position to do this two or three times a year because we are in their area more frequently to visit family, attend a conference, or do something of that nature. Minimally, however, we should meet face-to-face with our partners at least once a year.

If we have partners scattered from Kansas City to Canada and from California to Florida, then it may be more difficult to see every one of those partners each year. In this situation, we could make it a goal to see as many of them as we can, but we might have to accept seeing them every second or third year. If we are serving in a foreign country, then it may be best to try to see them every two years. In between, we can strengthen the communication with FaceTime, Skype, videos, or any other type of audio/visual method. Otherwise, we plan visits as often as possible.

The visit provides us with an excellent opportunity to walk in love—to encourage and minister to our partners. This is our opportunity to share the stories and achievements of what has been taking place in our lives and ministry. And this is their opportunity to see how partnering with us is producing fruit for the kingdom of God. It is also a great way to say *thank you*, and to share stories and accomplishments of what God has been doing since the last time we connected.

When we meet together with our partners, we want part of our focus to be briefing them on what has happened over the past year, while the other half of the meeting needs to be spent clarifying the vision for the upcoming year. Like a football team, whose players huddle and call plays, we meet face-to-face to review the year and then plan for what comes next.

Unfortunately, many people who support missionaries never see them face-to-face. Maybe this meeting has taken place once to start the partnership, but then they can go years without seeing each other. We don't want to allow that to happen in our partnerships. Our visits are such a good time to strengthen relationships and draw the family of God together that we need to commit ourselves to making them happen.

Doing yearly visits is a perfect time to cast vision, share about the future, and invite our partners into increased involvement. One of the things we are going to do in our yearly visits is give them an opportunity to increase their giving, to share a special gift for a specific project, or to even host a special event for us to introduce us to their friends.

Another wonderful benefit of our yearly meetings is they provide us an opportunity to pray together. In fact, some visits may turn into prayer meetings. This has happened in so many of my meetings where we sat and prayed for one another. We may have a significant spiritual connection with our partners, and they can be greatly encouraged by us and the work we are doing. So we want to take time to pray for them and minister to them.

Where there is a lack of vision, we tend to lose focus and commitment. We forget why we are doing what we are doing. The same can be said for our partners, too. Remember, we always keep the vision in front of them and call them higher. We remind them of what they are doing as partakers in the ministry while always pointing to the future.

Always Be Prepared

Before each yearly meeting with partners, we should take a moment to review information about our team members. I like to keep a journal or notebook of information about the people I meet—names, children's names, how long they have been believers, their church background, where they work, family history, and so on. Keeping notes on the people I meet, and reviewing that information right before a meeting with them, helps keep their lives and interests fresh in my mind. We can also do the same before connecting with them on the phone.

Before we go into our face-to-face meeting to share with our partners, we need to know what we are going to ask for and why. I make it a point to ask something every time I am there. It's going to be about special gifts, excited friends, or an increase in their partnership giving, and it will *always* include a prayer assignment. (I ask for one of these three things in each yearly meeting. I don't ask for all three in the same meeting.) We must be prepared to respond and follow through on our request. For the prayer assignment, I type it out on a card and have ready to hand it to them. I also have a notebook and pen ready to take down the contact information of excited friends they may suggest. As we can see, it is important to think it through before we go. We need to plan, asking ourselves, "What am I going to ask my partners to do? What am I doing this coming year that they would really be interested in getting behind?" Then we prepare ourselves and materials accordingly.

Like any other meeting, we want to be sure to have all our materials and gifts in order to be ready to share. All our materials need to be updated before we leave on our trip. For example, if we are using photos and brochures, they should be updated every other year. We don't want to use photos on brochures that are six or seven years old. We also want to have some materials and resources with us that cast vision for our work. Whether it's a CD, book, or pamphlet, we want to have those available as they actually help our partners gain an appreciation for the type of work we do and the people we minister to. For example, if we minister to orphans in Eastern Europe, we may want to share a book on God's heart for the orphan. If we reach out to the lost in the Middle East, we may want to share a book about God's heart for the nations.

It is so important to think through the whole appointment—greeting, sharing stories and testimonies, vision casting, extending invitations, and so on. So we should have our plan outlined for our meeting. This is only a general plan and outline to follow. Sometimes we can get a great plan, we will go into the meeting, and then the Holy Spirit throws it right out the window! So to get the most said and done, and the most vision casting with encouragement, we want to think it through beforehand—have a plan, have an outline, and roll with it.

Before we go, we ought to look at their giving report from our records. It needs to be updated before we go into the meeting. This can be a really valuable tool of encouragement. In other words, we can say, "Mr. Johnson, do you realize that in this past year of our partnership you have sown two thousand and two hundred dollars into our ministry? Thank you very much!" That record should be available to us, so we should have that information at our fingertips—know how we are going to share it and how we are going to refer to it.

Let's not forget the logistics of the meeting. We want to make sure we have a clear meeting time and location. We may want to send a reminder or appointment confirmation via text, or maybe we choose to email them a couple of days beforehand. We want to stay on top of these things, for failing to plan is a plan for failure.

When Meeting with Partners

THINK ABOUT OUR GREETING

We want to know how we are going to greet our partners and what we are going to say in those first couple of minutes as we walk right inside their door. They may have been friends for ten years, and greeting them may be a lot easier and more organic, but they could be people we only met six weeks ago. Either way, it is important to have a plan and think through how we are going to greet them. Like most everything else in partnership development, we don't just figure it out on the fly.

Making the first ten minutes or so all about them can help put them at ease, and it can also help calm our nerves. I would recommend asking them about their family, their work, what's going on at their church, or their hobbies and interests. This is where taking notes from previous meetings can come in handy. We want to refer to those notes as we prepare for our times of greeting and small talk.

It may also be helpful to have a short list of questions ready to fan conversation. For example, if I don't have much natural relationship with these particular partners yet, then I might have four or five go-to questions I can ask them at any point in the meeting. This helps conversation move along, and I don't get caught in awkward airtime.

Again, as always, we try to make this as natural as possible. All of this is just part of loving our neighbor like we love ourselves. It should also help set a comfortable tone for the meeting as well. If we are really walking out the second greatest commandment to love, then we are going to listen and ask questions. We are going to pray and be interested in what's going on with our partners.

ACKNOWLEDGE THEIR PARTNERSHIP

I cannot emphasize this enough: we always say *thank you*. We mention their willingness to give and how encouraged we are by their contributions and partnership. They have ten thousand other places they could be supporting, but they have chosen to give to us and our ministry. Our thank-you should include how their giving touches us personally, as well as how it impacts the overall ministry. Seeing us feel encouraged and blessed helps them feel more like a part of the team.

Our thank-you should also include some of the practical aspects: "I could not share the love of Christ with Brazilian street kids without your partnership." Developing a partnership team means we learn how to say *thank you* well and say it often. We can say a thank-you that really encourages our partners and calls them higher, or we can also say *thank you* in a way that makes them feel uncomfortable. If we do it with sincerity, vision casting, accomplishment, and achievement, then we will do well.

Sharing a testimony of an impact we have made through their partnership, how we were thinking of them, and how grateful we are for their partnership are all great ways to connect them with the overall vision. So we will want a couple of go-to stories that have happened over the past year: testimonies, healings, and breakthroughs. If we can, we should share the people's names and actual places, giving the details and painting a picture that glorifies God and brings the stories and events to life.

SHARE ACCOMPLISHMENTS

The persons we are sitting down with partner with us because of the vision God has put on our hearts. This is our chance to give that to them and update them about all that has been going on in our lives. Vision will evolve as time goes on, so we need to include them in that. We can do this by giving them a review of the past year, sharing testimonies and stories. We can't get all the communication in our newsletters and the occasional postcard or phone call, so we share more with them here about what was accomplished this last year. Let's draw them into the story, show-ing them how their partnership has made the story possible and telling them in detail what their giving has accomplished.

CAST VISION FOR THE FUTURE

One of our goals here is to share with them the vision God has given us for the upcoming year. We should share a little of the journey and how we arrived there, how the Lord has led us thus far. Then we can break down our plans into two or three steps or into seasons or calendar quarters. This will help them see that we have thought it through, that we are following the Lord's direc-tion, and that we are being a good steward of His calling.

We may want to say something like, "This year we feel like the Lord has said a, b, c, d, and e to us, and we want to get it done. So our plan to get there in this first quarter is to focus on a and b. In the second quarter we are going to focus on c. Then in the third quarter we are going to focus on d and e." In other words, we don't say it so generically that they question whether it is ever going to get done. We break it down a little and explain it to them in steps. This will show them that we have thought it through, that we have a plan, and that we are going to execute it.

Let's not forget to invite them to join us in the journey through prayer. We want to have our prayer card handy to share with them. It ought to cover the next three months. Our prayer card should have points concerning the vision we just cast. It should not be overly general but specific to the vision and the plans we are trying to accomplish for the upcoming year. We need to ensure we include a specific request on the card and then update that card every quarter. It is really difficult for someone to carry a prayer assignment every day for five, six, or seven months at a time. So we update them as things change—prayers get answered, new needs arise, or vision becomes more specific.

ASK FOR MORE INVOLVEMENT

Every yearly meeting with partners should include some kind of an ask. We don't need to shy away from the ask; instead, we want to use it to draw them further into our ministry. We want to develop them into a more involved partner. We all grow in our giving just as we all grow in our Christianity. This is a way to help them grow as those who have sent us into the mission field. Doing this on a regular basis helps keep the partnership from getting stale. Additional asks provide an opportunity for stewardship along with greater involvement.

We could consider asking them for an increase in giving at these yearly meetings. In most households, the economics change about every two and a half years. There is a pay raise, a car is paid off, the kids are out of school, the kids got their braces off, one of the missionaries they support is no longer in missions, etc. Many are happy to give more when they are able to. Now that they have a little bit more money to work with, they are happy to increase their giving. Additionally, the American cost of living goes up about 3 percent every year. That means it costs more to live and it costs more to do ministry than it did a year ago.

Our ministry is also growing, and the economy is always changing. There is always a need to increase our salary just to keep up with the cost of living expenses. Many partners will respond happily if we ask them to do so. I do it at the end of a meeting as a sort of takeaway point: "Hey Jim, Janice, I want to invite you to consider increasing your giving this year. We are growing the ministry, we are doing a, b, and c, and we are going to need an increased salary. We are inviting team members to increase their giving by 10 to 15 percent in this coming year to help us reach our goals. Would you take a couple of weeks to pray about that and I will follow up later with you, and see what you have decided?"

Also, it is good to ask for a special gift. I don't say "one-time gift"; rather, I refer to it as a special gift. This type of ask should only be done if the vision cast has been done first. Be sure to share the amounts, timelines, and dates the funds are needed by. In other words, if I am going to ask for a special gift, it is toward a particular project. I am going to share about the project; I am going to cast vision about the project; I am going to share the desires, goals, and how God has led me concerning this project; and I am going to share what the project is going to cost. Then I will ask them to share a special gift.

Another thing I will ask for from time to time is excited friends. This is really a personal recommendation from one friend to another. We make personal recommendations to our friends all the time: restaurants, doctors, mechanics, books, and movies. We do things in life, we enjoy them, and we have friends we think would enjoy them also, so we happily recommend them to our friends. The issue with ministry is no different. I have been blessed by so many books and CDs because a friend recommended them to me. This is much of what we are doing: I will take the time to ask my partners about meeting their friends. Again, I will ask for one of these three things in each yearly visit—not all three at the same visit.

LET'S PRAY FOR THEM

Every meeting should include prayer at some point and time. The right time to pray may be at the beginning, during the middle, or it may be at the end of the meeting. Small talk might present the opportunity when we first arrive and meet with the person. Usually, however, it will be at the end, but we should remain open to the Holy Spirit and follow His leading.

At any point in the conversation, if the Holy Spirit highlights something, we take a moment to pray. Maybe at the end of our meeting we can ask them if there is anything we can pray for. So we pray for them right then and there. We don't want to forget to write that prayer request so we can continue to pray for them after the meeting is over.

MAKE ROOM FOR GOOD FELLOWSHIP

Making room for good fellowship can be done at the beginning, during the extended small-talk time, or toward the end of the meeting. We must not forget its importance to our relationship with our partners. We don't want to be so locked into our outline that we forget to be a friend. Being a friend is important, and loving them is our joy and responsibility! This helps bring an organic nature to our meeting. Besides, it is an opportunity for enjoying each other as we hang out and interact.

The fellowship should be organic, fitting in where it naturally flows. We do this every day with our friends, and we know how to do it. So let's just be a friend and be natural. If we are a dinner guest in their home, we can ask them what they would like us to bring. If it's a more casual meeting, we can consider taking a little treat of some kind that we can share. We do want to remain sensitive to their time and schedule, though. We want to fellowship well but not overstay our welcome. It's good to learn how to depart gracefully.

Lapse in Partnership

A lapse in giving is something that does happen on occasion. We may have partners who forget to send a gift or who just stop sending in their gift altogether. What do we do when this happens?

First, it is important to keep track of everyone's giving, and when we see they have missed a month, we make a note of it. I use a hard copy spreadsheet with everyone's names and amounts recorded on it. (Please feel free to use whatever software, sheet, or program works for you.) It covers the course of a month. I have a different sheet for each month in a three-ring binder. When the gift comes in, I highlight it. Then at the end of the month, if there is a blank spot that hasn't been highlighted, I can clearly see those who didn't send in their gifts. When I flip over to the next page and start another month, I will fill it out in the same way. At the end of that second month, if these partners haven't given in the past two months, then I will call them.

I assume that something has kept them from sending in their gift. Maybe there are problems with their job, health, family, or something of a similar nature. I go low, assuming that there has been a problem, and I seek to be pastoral in this situation, not trying to find out why they aren't supporting me.

When I get on the phone with them, I ask if everything is all right, if everything is okay with their job, family, and health. They might say, "Hey, why do you ask?" Then I will say, "You have been such a great partner, so consistent in your giving, and when I noticed you had missed the last two months, I assumed something had kept you from it. Maybe there was a problem at home or financially, and I just wanted to catch up with you and see if there was any way I could pray for you."

Now, when this happens, most of the time I find out they forgot, and they are a little embarrassed. But because I went low and did it in humility, the situation is easily remedied. On occasion, we will find out there really was a problem—financial, health, or marital. Because we will go in low and in humility, we have a great opportunity to minister to our partners. We want to approach our interaction with them under the assumption that something has kept them from giving. We wouldn't have an opportunity here if we didn't keep good records and didn't stay attuned to whether or not our partners have lapsed in their giving. So we want to remember to keep good records and stay on top of them.

I want to mention another thing here that I believe is important. I don't call my partners after one missed gift. No, I wait until they have missed two months in a row. Sometimes people will miss a month, but once I see they have missed the second month, I figure it is possible something could be wrong. I don't wait until three or four months have passed by, because that actually makes it more awkward. We must get on the phone quickly and catch it. If they did lose a job and took a dramatic cut in pay, we should offer a reduced amount as a possible solution. We will have to play this situation by ear and be sensitive to the Holy Spirit. I would rather keep them engaged at a lesser amount than have them drop their giving altogether.

However, there are situations that might actually call for them to completely stop their partnership. If this is the case, we acknowledge what they have done in the past—sharing accomplishments and achievements—and we then encourage them, seeking to be a blessing to them. We can continue to reach out to them with continued communication like the newsletter and thereby keep the door open for the future. In other words, we might have to postpone that partnership momentarily, but we end it on a good note and with a great relationship. We continue our connection, then, through the newsletter. We can keep in mind that we may be able to revisit that partnership at a later date.

Conclusion

Hopefully, we can see the importance of yearly visits with our partners. They are great times to express thanks for all our partners have done over the past year, to cast vision about the upcoming year, and to share prayer requests and needs. Not only is the yearly visit a great way to continue to develop our partnership, but it is also a great way to fulfill Jesus' second greatest commandment: to love our neighbor as ourselves.

Looking Inside

- What are some ways you can help someone grow in their heart for giving?

- What are some ways that you can help people grow in the area of missions?

- What are some books, testimonies, articles, or websites that you could share to increase someone's understanding of God's heart for the nations?

Taking Action

1. Having a good contact management system will be very important. There are several CRMs (client relationship management) on the Internet. Some are free, and some come loaded with features for a small monthly fee. One of my favorites is *Insightly*. There is also a free program available online for download called *tntMPD*, which was created by missionaries for missionaries. It is a very powerful, helpful tool. Do some internet research on CRMs, including *tntMPD* and *Insightly*.

2. Choose a CRM and begin to enter all of your contacts and their information.

CHAPTER FIFTEEN

Love Our Team Well

Appreciate, encourage, inform, inspire, and cast vision.

When we get to the end of our partnership development campaign, we will have added people who are now co-laboring with us in full-time ministry. Learning how to communicate well and often with our partnership team must become a priority as we do the work of the ministry.

In this chapter, we will cover the DNA of a ministry lifestyle, how often we should say *thank you* to our partners, what good communication looks like, and how to write our monthly newsletter. The aim of this chapter is to provide concepts and some details that will strengthen the team of people with whom we are running this race.

Now What?

Many who have done well this far stumble in the area of partner care. Why is that? It could be because of fear, lack of training, poor planning, ignorance, or any number of other reasons. But I think the main reason most people stumble in this area is due to the lack of a plan. As we have said many times throughout this book, every goal needs a plan. In this particular context, keeping our team for the long term is the goal.

I liken keeping our team to a car that is in motion. It takes a lot of time, energy, effort, and hard work to get a parked car moving. But once it is moving, it is easier to keep it moving. The same can be said with our partnership team. We are going to spend a good deal of time, labor, and energy team-building in this heightened, focused season of our campaign. But now that we have worked hard to gather a team, it is not as hard to keep our team—but we do need a plan.

We will need to determine the level of relationship we want with our team, what it takes to love well, and then we can look at the amount of contact we need to have with our team—conversations, newsletters, visits, and so forth. Once we decide the level of contact we need with them, then we need to break it up into a daily, weekly, and a monthly schedule. We will need to write it down. A detailed plan, outline, and schedule should be worked into our calendar so that every day our calendar is already telling us what to do for our partners.

We want to love well. If we can get this one concept into our thinking as we approach our team, many problems will be taken care of in a very natural, organic way. Regardless of being a missionary called to full-time ministry, or that we profess the name of Jesus and we are believers, we have a lifestyle that *requires* us to love well. Our team is made up of our brothers and sisters. They are not just a financial means to an end, and they are *not* an ATM. They are brothers and sisters whom we want to love accordingly. Ministry is always about people, including the ones on our team. There is no ministry on Earth that is as important as loving people.

This all really comes down to what it means to walk in love. Regardless of our occupation or our time in the kingdom, we never graduate from this very basic need to love well. Our team is to be just as much the recipients of our ministry and love, kind words and encouragement, as the people to whom we are ministering occupationally.

Have a Plan

Once again, we need to have a plan or system in place if we are going to keep our team. Here is a little bit of what I do, but it can be adjusted and tweaked for other situations.

When it comes to acknowledging all gifts, I have a system: all the gifts that come to our ministry are mailed to a P.O. Box. (Organizations may have a different requirement for where gifts are sent.) Before I take them to the business office, I acknowledge all giving by first recording it in a ledger and then immediately responding to the sender with a thank-you. I stick to the plan. It has become a normal part of what I do. I acknowledge gifts as quickly as possible.

To keep things creative, I use emails, postcards, phone calls, or possibly what I call personal messages—either texting or via Facebook—that I rotate through on a consistent basis. I pull from that list, and it helps me shape how I want to say *thank you* each time—in a slightly different way. Some of the thank-yous are simply that; they just say *thank you*. But others show appreciation, cast vision, or share achievement.

Our pattern could be two emails, then a postcard, then a phone call. Which means one month when they send in money, we send an email thanking them for their gift. The next month when they send it in, we send another email acknowledging their gift. The third month, we send them a personally written postcard to thank them. Then every four months or so, they are getting a personal phone call from us, thanking them for their gift. By the end of the year, our team has heard from us for just about every gift, and our partners haven't received a series of redundant thank-you notes having been sent to them in the same way. Instead, thank you has been expressed in different ways: with vision casting, sharing appreciation, and sharing achievements, all through different mediums.

At the end of the year, everyone has been thanked and has heard from us outside of our regular newsletter. They have also received a couple of handwritten cards from us as well as a couple of phone calls. That is a good amount of contact, even if we just do it around the thank-you.

DNA of Team Relationship

ACKNOWLEDGE ALL GIVING

We want to try to acknowledge every gift as fast as we can. If we do not say *thank you* within twenty-four hours, then it's the same as not saying *thank you* at all. It is like a belated birthday card. The thank-you loses its punch and specialness if we wait too long. So if we have those gifts sent to a P.O. Box or a payroll system, then we should check it regularly and acknowledge all gifts as quickly as we can.

SHOW APPRECIATION

We need to tell our partners how much we appreciate them, their friendship, and their partnership. We must show them that we care about them as people and that we are grateful for their relationship and partnership. One of the reasons I do this is because it is part of walking in love. But secondly, I want them to know that I care about them and that it isn't just about the money. Thirdly, if the financial partnership ends someday, I already have a great friend, and I can continue the friendship I have formed long after the financial partnership is done.

We show appreciation in writing, by phone, and by a personal message. I think it's a good idea to occasionally send a card out of the blue, telling them how much we appreciate them as well. We can even phone them and just say, "Hey, I wanted to call you to see how I could pray for you. I really appreciate you!" We want to speak encouragement and blessing to them, mentioning the gifts we see in them. We want to show appreciation to them as people, not just as partners.

When we do our regular visits with our existing team, we may take a small gift. We don't have to do this in order to show appreciation, but it is just one way that we *can* show appreciation. If we do take a gift, we want it to be personal, showing thought and appreciation. In other words, if we have thirty-five people on our team and we are going to see all thirty-five during a two-week trip in the spring, we don't take them all the same CD or the same book. If we can, we should observe their individuality and their lifestyle in both the gift we bring them and the way in which we communicate with them. We try to determine what kind of person they are, what they like, their habits, their tastes, etc., and then we share a gift that is appropriate for that person. In sharing a gift, if I don't think I can do that or it is going to be too expensive by the time I buy everyone on my team a gift, then I choose to show them appreciation in a different manner.

Birthdays and anniversaries are great times to show appreciation and to speak a blessing over them. There are software programs that will alert us to things like that if we take a few moments to record their information. It would be nice to send it so that it arrives the day before their birthday—or if we call them, we can call the day or night before. The reason is that *on* their birthday they are going to get bombarded all at once by Facebook messages and other people calling them to wish them happy birthday. If we do it the day before, it will be unique and possibly stand out to them.

Another way we can show appreciation is to consider helping our partners in a practical way. Maybe they are moving or maybe they are painting their house when we are in town. Whatever they are doing—we help them. We could host them in our city, help them coordinate a short-term missions trip with our organization, or arrange for them to receive personal prayer ministry. In my years of missions work and training in partnership (as well as coaching missionaries), it is my experience that 60 to 70 percent of the people who stopped supporting a missionary did so because they believed the person was not grateful or did not appreciate them as a person. We want to live in a way that we will *never be accused* of these two things.

SHARE ACCOMPLISHMENTS

It is important that we remind our team from time to time what their partnership accomplishes. They need to hear about the fruit we are seeing as a result of their partnership. Hearing about how God was working through us was one of the reasons they decided to partner with us in the first place. They wanted to make a difference. It is important that we share testimonies, stories, videos, letters, and phone calls. When we do this, it helps them connect their partnership to the fruit. "Because of your partnership, I was able to go serve full-time today and two people heard the gospel. They thank you, and I thank you."

A newsletter solely dedicated to sharing achievements once or twice a year is a really good idea. In other words, the whole letter itself isn't just current events of the previous month or what we plan to do next month, but we might think about writing one entire letter about what we and our partners achieved together in that year.

Or possibly we can consider sharing achievements in the last paragraph of our newsletter every month. Maybe I wrote about an outreach through the whole letter, but sometime at the end I mentioned what my partners and I are accomplishing and achieving together. I thank them for it. I weave that into the thank-you notes, into postcards, and sometimes even into phone calls. That's what I mean by that underlying current running through our ministry. It is the DNA. It is the lifestyle of our life as a missionary—showing love and appreciation.

CAST VISION

God created us to respond to vision, but if we don't have a vision before us, if we are not reminded of where we are going and why we do what we do, we will forget it and begin to cast off restraint. When we lose our vision, that constraint begins to loosen and we cast it off. When our partners begin to lose vision about us, our ministry, and why they are involved, they will stop praying for us and, eventually, stop giving. When we keep our vision in front of them, their hearts are stimulated and they stay engaged.

Any vision we have should always be connected to God's global plan. I say this often, but it bears repeating: God is the original missionary. There is really only one mission at work in the earth, and that is the restoration of all things; everything else is a supporting role to God's ultimate plan. It is important that we have this understanding, it's important that we communicate this principle on occasion, and it's important that our people understand that all ministry is going in a particular direction. In other words, we don't become so myopic in our own ministry that we (and they) lose connection with the bigger picture.

SHARE FUTURE PLANS

We can share about upcoming events in a newsletter. At the end of the year, when we write the "ask letter," we can talk about the future year that is coming and our plans for it. We can share about ministry trips, dates, and deadlines that we are working toward, and any outreach events. Some of this we may need to raise additional funds for, and we could talk about it in a separate communication. Maybe we have a little text box in our newsletter titled, "Upcoming Events," and we can put little blurbs in there, little bullet points. Then, as the event approaches, we could talk about it in more detail. On our yearly visits, we can sit down with them and tell them what we have planned for the coming year.

Communications

Two key components to successful partnership—both in building our team and in keeping our team—are communication and relationship. Since there are multiple means of communication and different mediums, we need to know which one works best for particular people and situations. Let's not be fooled: not every medium always works because it is convenient. We want to use the right mediums for the right situations.

We put a communication plan in place, of which consistency is vital. We create a contact plan, looking at our contacts and breaking them down into categories and then into groups A, B, and C. We need to select the type of communication we want to have with each of those groups by the end of the year, and then break that communication up into smaller segments and create a schedule. In this way, every week we can sit down and have one or two hours focused on communication. In that window of time, we look at our schedule, look at our plan, follow the steps, and do what our chart tells us to do.

Here are a couple of things to consider in our communication process:

Remain proactive. In other words, we should call, we should follow up, we should start the conversation, and we should take the initiative in our communication and relationship. We don't sit around waiting for someone to call us. When it comes to sharing information with our partners, it is best to choose the medium that best suits the need. I am not going to write in a newsletter about a cool website that I have started and give my partners a link to visit that page; rather, I would include that on Facebook or in an email. When they open up their email, they will only get one or two sentences of introduction, and then they can immediately click on a link. They shouldn't have to search for the information I am sending them. We want to make things really easy for them.

Consider sharing pictures with them through something like Picasa or other picture sharing websites using a short email of explanation. One of the reasons I do this is to not clutter my newsletter with a bunch of pictures. I would rather talk and share the vision God has given me with words than use a lot of pictures. Pictures are fine, but most of the time I find they are overused in a newsletter. We could upload our pictures on a picture sharing website, and then send out an email telling our partners about it with a link to the pictures.

Consider sharing short videos with them from time to time. We want to make it a decent, quality video, if we do it. It doesn't have to be high definition taken with a five-thousand-dollar-camera, but it does need to be done well. If we are going to use just a cell phone, we can place it on a tripod to hold it steady. If we are videoing outside, we can put something over the microphone to cut down the wind noise. So we want to put some time into it, rehearse it, have an outline, and know what we are going to say before we record it. The goal is to make a good, quality video with good sound. A video can be an effective and quick way to communicate with our team.

Newsletters

I know it sounds rather cliché, but the number one goal of writing a newsletter is to get it read. We want to do everything we can to help this letter get read. We should want it to be short, clear, encouraging, and real—containing actual news and not a bunch of fluff.

Our monthly newsletter is the most important part of our partnership team. It's the main place we go to connect and talk to our partners on a monthly basis, our most vital tool in this relationship. It is our main point of contact, and therefore we don't want to skip it or rush through it. We need to take the time to make it a good letter. In other words, because of the importance of this communication tool, we will want it to be good communication that our partners look forward to receiving, that they are happy to open up, and that actually says something that is worth reading.

Our newsletter is an important communication tool, providing an excellent opportunity for us to share about the exciting things God is doing. Therefore, I want to be sure the letter is read, and one thing I can do to help ensure its reading is to send a hard, paper copy. In our digital age, where we are bombarded with emails, it has been my experience that less than 50 percent of mass emails are actually opened. This isn't successful communication.

For my financial and prayer partners, and about another fifteen to twenty key people, I send a hard-copy newsletter. So let's use the hard copy for our partnership endeavors.

If I feel that I have to write a two- or three-page letter that looks like a magazine spread every month, it won't get done. The short, concise letter is something I can be faithful to. If it's one page, partners are more likely to open it and read it. If they get overwhelmed with a volume of text and a multitude of different things going on at once, then they are going to set it aside and not read it. So I try to make it short and easy on the eye.

I often hear this from missionaries: "I don't know how to find the balance of ministry, personal, and fun." I recommend only picking one topic and writing about that one thing—that is it. If I am using one page with a minimal amount of pictures—sometimes I don't even use a picture—then that is going to be around four hundred words. If I am only writing about one topic, it is amazing what I can get said in just that small number of words.

Not only do I write about one topic, but I try to address each letter to one person. To do this, I pretend that I am writing to only one recipient of the letter. I don't call him out by name, though. In other words, I don't talk to Jim all throughout the letter. But what I will do is pretend that there is one recipient, one person who will read this letter. I will use phrases like "you" instead of "as you all know" or "as many of you know." That is automatically putting them in a group, putting them on a list, and not something I want to do. Doing this makes the language become much more personal.

We need to take the time to make the newsletter interesting. I see two extremes in this area: most missionaries don't know what to write about, or they do know what they want to write about but they overstate it or give too much information. The other thing I see happen is that they really don't have anything to say and they try to say something anyway to validate their existence as a missionary. They try to show how much of an impact they are making and how awesome their ministry is when really, that month there just wasn't a whole lot of new stuff going on. We don't want to do this. When we have that type of month, we should write a personal newsletter about achievements thus far for the year.

We want to look for ways to emphasize the contribution of our partners to the ministry and their involvement in it. Let's help our partners see the difference they are making by partnering with us. We want to connect them to it through their encouragement, their gift, and the timeliness of their special gift or their prayer. We show them the fruit they are bearing through our ministry.

Our newsletter should have a consistent schedule. We should start writing it four or five days before we want to mail it out, and then we mail our letter out approximately the same time each month, whether it is on the first or the fifteenth. We decide what works best with our schedule, but we do that regularly and consistently. This is good for us, and it is good for them, creating in them an anticipation for our letter to show up at the same time each month.

One of the biggest mistakes we can make as missionaries is to be out of sight and out of mind. So let's not be out of sight! Our newsletter is a great way to stay connected with people. In it, we must include a thoughtful, good, and sincere thank-you.

I do not recommend including financial needs in a monthly newsletter. Our monthly newsletter should be exciting, encouraging, and fun, so we don't share our financial needs in it, we don't ask for funds, and we don't drop hints, hoping people will understand and send extra money that month. If we actually need financial help, then we ask, but we do it in a separate communication followed up by a phone call and then possibly followed up by a face-to-face ask.

Conclusion

In order to serve God long term in full-time ministry, we will not only need to build a partnership team, but we will love well those people who are now running together with us. The DNA of team relationships should include an acknowledgement of all giving, consistent appreciation, shared achievements, and regular vision casting and sharing future plans. Loving our team well means that we have a communication plan where we are consistently sharing with them through the most effective mediums.

The most powerful tool in our communication tool belt is our monthly paper newsletter. Our newsletter shouldn't read like multiple news clippings with frequent financial asks or shouldn't be cluttered with pictures. We will want it to be a personal correspondence with a ministry partner. The big-picture guideline for our newsletter is it needs to be one page, one-sided with one-inch margins, focused on one topic, and written with one person in mind. In our plan of consistent communication with our partnership team, we should include a yearly visit where we say thanks, acknowledge their partnership, cast vision, and present a clear ask.

Looking Inside

- If your giving was making a real impact and a missionary was letting you know how, would you find this encouraging?

- Which would you appreciate more: someone wishing you a happy birthday via Facebook or a phone call with a prayer of blessing?

- No one dislikes appreciation. What are some creative ways you could acknowledge your partners in showing your appreciation for them and their gift?

- What are some things that make you feel appreciated?

Taking Action

1. Go online and search newsletter templates. There are hundreds of options to get you started. Most of them are for the business world but can be adjusted easily.

2. Next search for how to write a good newsletter. I have found almost everyone needs help; there are very few who are natural at writing good newsletters. The difference between a weak letter and a great one is just four

or five basic practices. Practice the following for a good newsletter.

- If you have a name of your ministry, put it at the top. I do encourage that you have a header or headline of some sort at the top.

- Have an interesting lead sentence or headline that captures the reader's attention.

- Include a personal address: "Dear John and Jane."

- Make short paragraphs of various lengths, not exceeding seven or eight lines of text.

- Use simple, direct sentences with short, accurate words which really help communicate more clearly.

- Include a handwritten note at the bottom of your letter. This P.S. is optional, but I do recommend that you write a P.S. two to four times a year.

- Do not request additional support. Absolutely no request for additional support of any kind is to be implied or made!

- Use a balance of ministry and personal communication throughout the year. Try a ratio of 2:1 or 3:1 between ministry and personal contact.

- Send newsletters consistently.

CHAPTER SIXTEEN

We Can Do It!

Thousands of missionaries are already doing it.

I have seen called workers from various walks of life be successful in the area of partnership development because it is a kingdom dynamic and the kingdom transcends every culture, personal background, economic situation, demographic, tradition, and personality type. What matters is that God has called us and missions is the family business. God has a team for us, and partnership development is a journey to discover His team.

Developing a financial partnership team is a lot of work, as we now can tell, that takes time and will require us to develop some new skills. The journey is a roller coaster ride; we will have our good days and our not so good days. But every call we make, every appointment we go to, and every thank-you card we write will be worth it. All of it will prepare us to walk out our calling long term.

At the time of this writing, I have trained a couple thousand missionaries in partnership development, working with nearly every demographic imaginable. One thing that is consistent with all the people I have worked with is that, when missionaries have faith that God will provide, have clarity of vision, have a strategy, a plan, operate in best practices, stick to the model, and remain diligent, they are successful. It doesn't take a special kind of person to make this work; rather, it takes faith, strategy, diligence, and flexibility.

I know one of the best ways we are encouraged in our walks of faith is by hearing the testimonies of others who are doing or have done what we are attempting to do. So I want to share some testimonies to build our faith and understanding that we can do partnership development. I have personally talked with hundreds of missionaries over the years. Their stories are encouraging, and they have given permission to use them here. I have withheld their names to protect their identities. Like thousands of other missionaries that I have talked to over the years, we will see that these individuals realized they would have to make drastic changes if they were going to continue in ministry. Here are a few of their stories as told by them.

#1—Fully Funded while Serving on the Continent of Africa

"I grew up knowing God was asking me to give my life to full-time missions, and I was passionate about it. Africa, orphans, seeing Jesus' name made great, and prayer gripped my heart. I wanted to walk in the fullness God had for me. At twenty-one, I decided to jump into full-time ministry with both feet. It was six months into this new stage of life when I realized that I didn't want to do it without the support and partnership of other believers. I

also realized that I wouldn't be able to give myself wholly to what God was asking of me if I didn't have a means of income.

"I was living on savings, whatever babysitting jobs I could manage in between ministry, and the few random checks that would come from home. But one thing was clear: the money would soon run out. Either I had to find a way to be funded while in ministry, or I would have to quit and take up a "regular" job. The conviction of what God asked me to give my life to was so great and my passions so strong that it was obvious I wasn't going to quit, so I sought another way.

"In 2011, I committed myself to partnership development training. I was deeply impacted as I discovered more of God's heart for the Body of Christ to work together through partnership, with some going and others sending. I was thrilled to see this style of financial partnership woven all throughout Scripture, and I truly was excited to get out there and do it. After being trained on the practicality of all it entails, as well as taking adequate time to pray and prepare, I headed home for the summer to go on my first partnership campaign.

"I didn't go without setbacks, though. Having epilepsy not only prevented me from driving but it also forced me to be extremely flexible and persistent as I dealt with seizures and migraines. I was even hospitalized for part of the summer. There were some relational issues with someone who was close to me, throwing me for a loop. My summer was just a lot more emotionally draining than I planned going into my campaign, but I stuck with the plan. I wasn't getting the excited responses I had planned for either, and as I met with people, many told me they would have to get back with me about the possibility of partnering with me. But I chose to take my disappointment and frustrations to God. That summer I continually dialogued with Jesus about the call He had placed on my life and the team of people He desired to partner with me in this calling through prayer and financial support.

"Two-thirds of the way through my campaign, things started to change. I still had the stress of being unable to drive and the medical setbacks, but within weeks the yeses from people began to flood in. In about a matter of two weeks, I had just about reached my financial goal. Not only that, but I gained confidence in my vision as I watched the Holy Spirit move on people as they jumped on board with what God was doing through my life. I had made many new friends when people I met with introduced me to their friends who ended up partnering with me. My heart felt like it would explode as I watched God build a team of committed givers and prayer warriors who wanted to be a part of the calling He had given me.

"I am three years into living life as a fully-funded missionary. I have a team of incredible believers around me who truly have become like family to me. Their consistent giving, notes of encouragement, and beautiful friendships daily bless me and remind me of God's commitment to His plan for my life. My team shares with me how encouraged they are by my newsletters and the chance to pour into what God is doing. I no longer stress about finances, but I am able to give myself completely to all that God is asking of me. I live a modest but wonderful life and have the ability to sow into the lives of others as well.

"Being properly trained, working with a coach, raising up a partnership team, and continuing to maintain that team have completely changed the way I am able to say yes to the call of God on my life. God asked me to give myself to serving the fatherless and the continent of Africa, and to make His name great among the nations. Because of partnership, I am able to do that now, and I will be able to continue serving Him all my days."

#2—Fourteen Years into Missions, God Radically Shifted My Worldview

"In the months leading up to 1999, the Lord began to stir my heart and my wife's as well, about serving Him in full-time ministry. We didn't know what that would look like at the time, but it eventually became clear to us that it would be in missions. I was working in a full-time marketplace job with a technology company, maintaining websites and doing data entry. It was a great job at the time, but still being in the first year of marriage, we were unsure of how to provide for ourselves and still fulfill this longing God had put in our hearts.

"Even though we practically didn't know how it was all going to work out, we began to feel an urgency that this was the time we were to jump into ministry with both feet. We knew I would have to quit my job so that we could do this. My wife was working part-time then, so we were barely scraping by. But the cliff before us was how we were going to get funded. I went out and bought whatever books I could find on raising financial support. Up to that time, my only experience was sending out a letter, telling people about what

God had put on my heart, and then waiting to see who responded. There was not much of a response. We still had an urgency from the Lord, however, so we moved forward and, in a very unnecessary manner, scraped by for the next two years as we built a little team of six or seven solid people who were supporting us.

"With the increased costs of planning a family, and some other tentmaking avenues to make ends meet, which all took away and depleted us from what we were called to do, we sensed that something had to change. All the side businesses that were meant to fund our mission were ultimately not the way God wanted us to move forward. We were able to make ends meet with our calling in missions, but when we needed to put three of our children in school, we could see that this model wasn't sustainable. Something had to change.

"We were about fourteen years into missions. Living month to month distracted me from the vision God had given me, and I was living under the emotional stress and pressure of not knowing if I would be able to continue serving God full-time. We were paying our bills, but we were not saving or investing for our future. The issue wasn't that I didn't know what to do—I knew beyond a shadow of a doubt that God had called us—but with this stressed out, underfunded, distracted, overworked cycle, we could not continue to serve the calling of God on our lives. We needed to prioritize; we needed a long-term approach.

"That's when we had some partners inform us they were going to have to remove their partnership, and they let us know about six months in advance. And another one of our supplemental income strings was going to be gone in about six months as well. The loss of these two sources of income totaled about two thousand dollars a month, which forced us to make an adjustment and figure out how to raise a real partnership team.

"At that point, I went through formal partnership training, which laid the foundation for partnership and gave me some strategy on how to do it. Even though the last fourteen years were full of God's mercy, covering up our oversights, it still didn't seem like God's preferred way. When I went to the training, I realized I had a lot of ideas that were completely wrong about partnership. I know that, when God calls a person, He has an intention to fund that person. But what I didn't understand was the role human partnership plays in the way God chooses to fund those He has called. Through partnership training, we began to see that our scraping by was not the best way, nor was it God's intended way to fund us in what He had called us to do.

"I was shocked by how many wrong ideas I had about money and partnership, and how those ideas had a negative impact on my heart and on the ministry assignment God had given me. I didn't realize how much God cared for His own mission and how much He wanted to provide for us. There are so many benefits that took place as I grew in God's idea of partnership, as I grew in relationship with others, and in God's heart as well. It was encouraging because I knew there was a better way, but it was also discouraging because I was uncomfortable with what it required of me.

"I began to set apart time to do the things that were necessary to raise up partners. I began to clarify my vision—what I was doing, why I was doing what I was doing, and how to communicate it clearly and effectively. It wasn't that I began to implement a new model, but my worldview had completely shifted. I saw God's zeal for missions, and I was convinced that partnering with others was the way God wanted it done. In response to what I learned, I began to make changes. The process was uncomfortable, which was expected, but it was also needful. There is a wrong idea that just because God calls you, equips you, and changes your mind about partnership development, that it is going to be a Disney World ride. The journey was a bit different than I anticipated, but it was a real growing process.

"Having a vision, sharing it, and inviting others into partnering with us is God's way. And we didn't have to be apologetic about the invitation either. It wasn't until I had the foundation of that vision clear—of His servants who were called to do what God called them to do—that I realized so much of my hesitancy in asking people to partner with us was due to the fact that certain aspects of my vision were not clear. I was shocked at how people were willing and waiting to be invited into partnership with the Lord. There were many people who knew what we were already doing, and they were waiting for us to invite them into it.

"My biggest challenge was how necessary it was to take the time and prepare for everything related to the process of supporting a partnership team. Material preparations and appointment preparations took the most time. But the nature of the endeavor is such that much preparation was needed in order to be effective. There is a direct relationship of the measure of our preparedness to our success. The more I prepared, the more relaxed I was—the more dialed down—and the clearer I was in my approach.

"*Life is much different now that we have been doing partnership development. After a season of focusing on it, there were some dramatic changes that took place. We got a number of new partners, and there were some surprising benefits that came as a result. Sometimes when God told us to do something, we didn't understand all the reasons why we were to do it. We saw fruit in our relationships with others, in our relationship with the Lord, and in our relationship as a family—the stress that was once present is no longer there.*

"*Another benefit is that I feel more connected to my own calling; the whole process solidified it in a much greater way. The response of partners joining with us was a yes and amen to God's calling and assignment on our lives. My biggest surprise, compared to the fourteen years of missions work we did prior, is that I now feel like everything I do in my ministry is just one part of a body, or one extension of a team because of my new bond with our partners. When I open my mouth and disciple someone, or when I stretch out my hand and pray for someone, I realize there is a large group standing behind me. Without a team, God's heart for that person I'm praying for would not be communicated in the same way.*

"*Developing a partnership team produced gratitude for the people partnering with me and gratitude to the Lord for how He is binding our hearts together in accomplishing His purposes in the earth today. I not only get to thank our partners for the money they send, but I get to thank them for letting us minister God's heart so we can bring forth fruitfulness together. If the Lord were to call us and make it clear that we weren't supposed to be in full-time ministry for one reason or another, then we would still be in full-time ministry by partnering with someone else.*

"Being a Bible student and instructor over the past fourteen years, nothing could replace looking page by page and story by story, through both the Old and New Testaments, through the lens of how God accomplishes His work. The simplicity of the Lord calling, the person responding, and then the way in which he or she walks it out by sharing the vision and inviting people to partner with him or her absolutely astonishes me."

#3—God Provides a House for Full-Time Missionaries

"My wife and I started our missions ministry in 2008. We arrived at our missions base having come from northern California, ready to jump into the unknown and feeling the call of God on our lives. We were very excited about what God was going to do. After going through the internship program, I soon became a full-time missionary, but it wasn't long before I ran into the hard reality that I didn't have the financial ability to continue doing what I felt the Lord had called me to do. That plagued and troubled me because I was already into the assignment when I found out I didn't have the financial ability to carry it out.

"Praying and seeking the Lord about how to practically carry out my assignment, I met with a person who had tremendous revelation regarding the way of ascertaining and getting the funding we needed in order to fully carry out what we were called to do. He didn't just have the gift of encouragement, like we think of

Barnabas in the Bible, encouraging others to do what they ought to be doing—even though that is needful in the Body of Christ—but he had biblical understanding and revelation. He had this not only about the way he was going to teach me to be fully funded, but in addition to that he understood the importance of saying yes to what the Lord has called each and every one of us to do. It was paradigm shifting, to say the least.

"One of the illustrations my friend uses that has stuck with me is that there is a scroll in heaven that the Son of Man is holding, with my name written on it. Jesus has given me an assignment to do while I am on this earth, then He held it out to me in the spirit realm, and He gave it to me when He called me to this place. That scroll is what He will ask me about when I stand before Him at the end of my life. On that day, the thing I will care about the most is if I did what was written on that scroll, and if I did it with a sincere heart. That was quite a revelation where the lightbulb went on. My assignment was something that Jesus deeply cared about.

"We can talk about raising up a partnership team and being fully funded, but the context that we are talking about is following in the footsteps of Jesus, doing the will of the Father, doing what we see the Father doing in this generation, and getting on board with that. But to make this practical and hit home, we have our needs. My wife and I moved into missions with only one child, but we now had three to take care of. We were renting a small place that was only about five minutes away from the mission base. God began to speak to us through a number of ways that He was going to give us a house.

"While God was speaking to us about this, I met with my friend again and explained to him all that was happening, and he began to teach me about how the Lord would have me to ask my partnership team for this extra money. They had already been supporting us and helping us meet our monthly budget, but he encouraged me to ask them to partner with us in this special time to be able to get this house. Every time I would meet with him, he would teach me more about partnership development—namely, that I could walk out the assignment God had given me, that I could be faithful to His call, and that I would be able to do what the Lord had called me to do in the long term.

"There are a lot of ideas about faith out there today, and a few of them seem to contradict this idea of going to people, sharing our vision, and asking people to partner with us. There's an idea that if we have faith, we don't have to take action on it because the Lord is going to provide for us—and there are times where we haven't asked anyone or told them our needs, and God moved on someone's heart to provide for us and give us a special gift. But the Lord really is in the business of partnership. We invite others into partnership because the Lord is into partnership, partnering with us in what He does in the earth. When we ask others to partner with us in what God has put in our hearts, we are linking arms with them. Faith is simply responding to what the Lord is doing and playing our part by sharing our vision and inviting others to partner with us as the Lord does His part in moving on people's hearts.

"My assignment in missions keeps me busy. I can't afford to be away for long periods of time. Not only that, but I have a wife and three kids at home, so I don't have the time or the luxury of being *away from my family for weeks on end either. The remarkable thing was that I could take a short trip, and God could use that to provide for our needs. I took a weeklong trip and met with almost every person on my partnership team, sharing with them what the Lord had been doing in our hearts and lives, and what it was that He had been speaking to us about.*

"I was amazed at their response. They were overjoyed and happy to partner with us, excited about what the Lord was doing. They sensed the call of God in the area of getting a house, and they began to lavishly and extravagantly sow into us. They jumped on board with what God was doing. After telling the story about what God had been doing, I invited them to partner with it. I returned from that trip with about thirty thousand dollars toward my house. This money was in addition to the down payment the Lord already had provided when He raised up another person who gave it to us. It was a brand new house, and it was completely outrageous that God would provide in such a way.

"We truly moved into full-time ministry with nothing, just my wife and our first child. God had told me that I was like Abraham, so I was to go to this land that I didn't know, and we went in obedience to the call of God. We never asked for a new house or for God to give us so much money toward it, but God was serious about this assignment. It was God's desire that we have what we needed to carry out the assignment. God truly is faithful to develop partners to work with His mission in our lives to walk out the call of God in our generation."

Conclusion

God doesn't fund personality types; He funds workers. Building a partnership team is not a new idea that we have just come up with. God has been funding His workers for almost four thousand years through the giving of the saints. If we are called into full-time ministry, then we can take comfort and confidence in this fact: God does not intend for us to do it alone; He wants His whole family engaged in His mission. We have made a commitment, and He wants others to make a commitment as well. God has a team for us.

Nobody knows our vision better than we do, and nobody can share it as well as we can. This is all we have to remember when it comes to partnership development: we receive a vision from the Lord, gather the people together, share what God has put on our hearts, and then invite the people to join us in that vision. We can do it!

My prayer for you is that you would have your mind renewed, that you would know, love, and embrace the simplistic beauty of partnership within the family of God. May He fill you with vision and faith, giving you grace to learn new skills and to meet new people. Be bold and be courageous!

May the following be your confession of faith. Read it aloud over yourself, several times a year.

My Statement of Faith

I have been called into full-time occupational ministry. I must respond by giving myself fully to this work; therefore, I will raise up the financial partnership team needed to accomplish my assignment. My obedience to Jesus is what really matters. Because I love Him, I will obey Him. My life is all I have to give. My life and ministry will bring glory to God.

God is willing and able to supply all the needs of my household and ministry, and He will primarily supply my needs through other people. There are people who, upon hearing about my assignment, will gladly partner with me. My ministry will be an answer to prayer for many; they have been praying for "laborers in the harvest," and here I am. I must move forward and discover the team He has prepared for me.

I cannot do God's part, and He will not do my part. Therefore, I will be excellent in all areas of ministry, starting with my partnership development. Raising the team that God has for me will be excellent training for ministry. I am not laboring in vain. Every hour I spend preparing, every piece of material I develop, and every appointment I go to will build character, teach me, train me, prepare me, and make me a better servant of the gospel. I will work hard; I will be diligent; I will stick to the strategy; I will always move forward; I will communicate clearly; I will articulate my assignment well; I will give it 100 percent and then allow God to do His part.

I am providing an excellent stewardship opportunity for the Body of Christ. I will not believe the lies of the devil. God has called me, and He has a team for me. I am developing a team for the sake of the gospel and for the glory of His name. There are plenty of resources for the task at hand; God would not commission me if there was not adequate supply.

My partnership team will mean much more than just finances. I will not treat them like an ATM, but rather as the brothers and sisters they are. I am determined to love them well. I will walk in the second commandment with everyone on my team and with everyone I meet. God is giving me real friends who understand partnership, and we will all work together to partner with Him in His global mission.

Father, thank You for my assignment, and thank You for the wisdom of biblical partnership.

ILLUSTRATION 1

Contact Process Chart

	Week 1	Week 2	Week 3	Week 4	Week 5	Week 6	Week 7	Week 8	Week 9
Group 1	Letter	Postcard	Phone Call	Appt.	Follow Up				
Group 2		Letter	Postcard	Phone Call	Appt.	Follow Up			
Group 3			Letter	Postcard	Phone Call	Appt.	Follow Up		
Group 4				Letter	Postcard	Phone Call	Appt.	Follow Up	

ILLUSTRATION 2

Contact Idea List

This list may help you brainstorm and remember people you actually do know. Look at each line and think through the categories.

- Accountant
- Advertising Agencies
- Apartment Manager
- Artists
- Auto Mechanic
- Avon Lady
- Baker
- Baseball Team
- Basketball Team
- Bank Personnel
- Barber
- Beautician
- Bible Bookstore Owner or Manager
- Bible Study or Prayer Group
- Boy or Girl Scout Leader
- Brother
- Building Contractors
- Butcher
- Children's Teachers
- Christian Business People
- Christmas Card List
- Church Choir Director
- Church Directory
- Church Friends
- Church Missions Committee

- Church Staff
- Civic Clubs
- Coaches
- Community Leaders
- Computer Programmers
- Corporate Executives
- Dentist
- Dental Assistant
- Doctor/Nurse/Office Staff
- Family Attorney
- Farmers/Ranchers
- Fast Food Restaurants
- Florist
- Former Customers
- Former Employees
- Former College Professors
- Former High School Teachers
- Former Salesman
- Former Roommates
- Foundations
- Fraternity
- Friends of the Family
- High School & College Friends
- House Church Networks
- Hospital Chaplains
- Hospital Personnel

- Insurance Agents
- Jaycees
- Kiwanis Club
- Mayor/Civic Leaders
- Men's Breakfast/Groups
- Military Personnel
- Missionary Societies
- Moms Groups
- Neighborhood Watch
- Neighbors/Former Neighbors
- Newspaper Personnel
- Parents
- Parents' Address Book
- Parents' Christmas Card List
- Parents' Employers
- Parents' Employees
- Parents' Business Contacts
- Pastors
- People You Have Led to Christ
- Prayer Chain
- PTA Organization
- Real Estate Agent
- Referrals
- Relatives
- Retired People
- School Activities
- Secretary/Receptionist
- Self-Employed Friends
- Service Men
- Shoe Salesman
- Sister
- Sunday School Class
- Tax Accountant
- Teammates
- Telephone Book
- TV and Radio Stations
- Veterinarian
- Yearbooks
- Wedding List
- Women's Clubs

ILLUSTRATION 3

Vision, Obstacles, Goals

Vision Statement

_____

_____

_____

What are *the top five obstacles* that stand in the way of your vision being fulfilled?

Examples may include the lack of training, finances, ailments, debt, lack of biblical understanding, family or personal circumstances, lack of a particular skill, fear, pride, lack of motivation, or lack of accountability.

1

2

3

4

5

OBSTACLE # _____

List the action steps to overcome this obstacle.

1. _____
   _____
   _____

2. _____
   _____
   _____

3. _____
   _____
   _____

4. _____
   _____
   _____

5. _____
   _____
   _____

ILLUSTRATION 4

Call Sheet

Group 1

Location: _____

	Name	Phone Number	Letter	Post-card	Phone Call	Appt Date/Time	Follow up	Results	Comments
1									
2									
3									
4									
5									
6									
7									
8									
9									

ILLUSTRATION 5

Letter Template

Get their attention. Use a catchy headline.

Dear Jim and Jane,

Paragraph 1: Bring them up to date.

Paragraph 2: Share your ministry calling and the story of how you were called.

Paragraph 3: Introduce your missions organization. Identify its vision and values.

Paragraph 4: Extend the invitation.

Blessings,

Your name

Don't forget to include a handwritten P.S.

ILLUSTRATION 6

Phone Call Outline

A. Greeting

- Let them know who you are.
- Make sure you have the person you want to talk to.
- Ask if it's a good time to talk. Respond accordingly, and set a time to call back if needed.
- Don't apologize for calling.

B. Small Talk (only for a few minutes)

- Review the person and your relationship before you call. Have a conversation point ready. Make small talk if you have the chance.
- Keep your ears open, and be sensitive to the Holy Spirit.
- Minister and pray when it's needed.
- Be a friend.

C. Purpose for Call

- Let them know why you are calling.
- Transition to asking for an appointment:
- "Hey John, the reason I am calling is that I recently sent you a letter sharing about our ministry . . . how God is moving in our lives and ABC ministries. Did you have a chance to read it?"

D. The Ask

- Ask them for an opportunity to talk and share more with them.
- If they say yes, express your appreciation and set a time, date, and location.

E. The Appointment

- Ask them for a time and place.

- If needed, let them know how long it will take (no more than one hour, unless their only availability is for a weekday lunch, then it might only be 30–40 minutes). Be flexible. Do what works for them.

- For people who feel too busy to meet, consider the following options for them (have a short list memorized and be ready to share when needed):

  - Dinner or a late dessert
  - Weekday breakfast (this works well for busy business people)
  - Business lunch
  - Evening coffee at a coffee shop
  - Sunday lunch after church or a brunch between services
  - A 40-minute appointment with a business person (possibly meet at their office)
  - A shorter meeting after small group, house church, or youth group where you would spend a few more minutes
  - If someone is going out of town, drive them to the airport—share on the way
  - Jump onto their schedule, run errands with them if you need to

F. The Confirmation

- Confirm the time, date, and location.
- Remember to speak it back to them.

ILLUSTRATION 7

Phone Call Flowchart

"Can I share with you in person?"

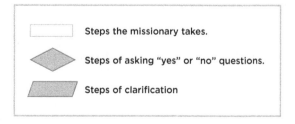

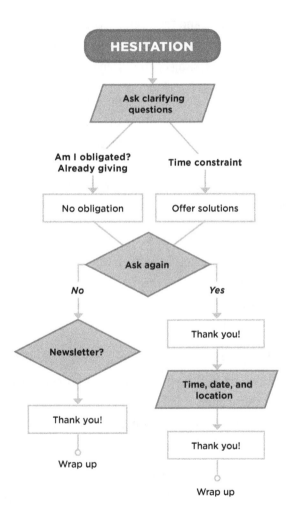

ILLUSTRATION 8

Appointment Outline

1. Greeting and small talk:

    - Ask about them and their family, their interests, hobbies, and their heart for missions. Try to ask a couple of questions about each subject and listen well.

2. Transition:

    - You can start your transition by saying, "John and Jane, thank you for meeting me here and giving me a chance to share with you about how the Lord has called me into ministry and how He is impacting students at XYZ University."

3. Bring them up to date:

    - Tell them where you have been and what you have been doing. You are bringing them up to date since the last time you talked with them. This would be a great time to share a recent testimony.

4. Talk about how you were called into full-time ministry:

    - Relate when and how the Lord started speaking to you about this calling.
    - Bring this part of the story up to the present, and be sure to share how the Lord has led you to this point.

5. Share the vision that God has given you:

    - Share your vision with excitement, conviction, clarity—and with a sincere heart. Be natural.

6. Talk a little about the missions organization you are working for:

   - Convey the overall vision of your missions organization.
   - Let them know when you will start full-time, if applicable.

7. Make room for questions

8. Invite them to partner with you:

   - Then take a short pause and transition with a restating of your vision/call in a sentence.
   - Do not hem-n-haw around, and don't look away. Look them right in the eye and say, "John and Jane, will you partner with me in ministry?" Continue to look them in the eye, and wait for the answer. Don't speak for them— let them be the next ones to talk.

9. Respond accordingly:

   - If they say *yes*, then say *thank you* and move toward wrapping up with the partnership card and the instructions for giving.
   - If they say *no*, try to discern the no. If it's a clear no, then move toward a special gift.
   - If they say a halfway yes, something like, "Well, I might . . . what would help you?" then share that you are asking the Lord to give you monthly partners.

10. The wrap-up

    - Thank them.
    - Give them a partnership card.
    - Give them the giving instructions.

11. Additional asks or excited friends if applicable

12. Fellowship

ILLUSTRATION 9

Appointment Flowchart

"Will you partner with me in ministry?"

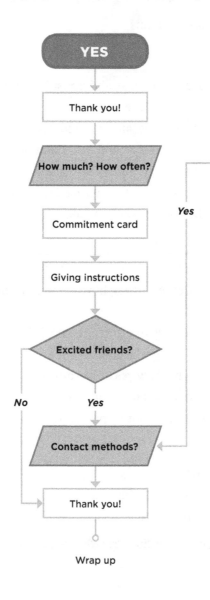

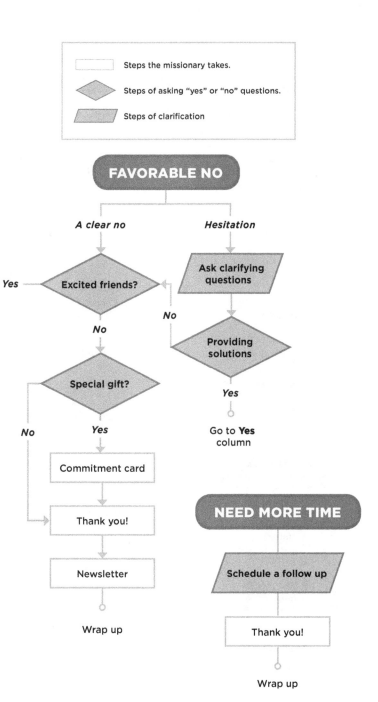

Steps the missionary takes.

Steps of asking "yes" or "no" questions.

Steps of clarification

FAVORABLE NO

A clear no

Hesitation

Ask clarifying questions

Yes

Excited friends?

No

No

Providing solutions

Special gift?

Yes

No

Yes

Go to **Yes** column

Commitment card

NEED MORE TIME

Thank you!

Schedule a follow up

Newsletter

Thank you!

Wrap up

Wrap up

ILLUSTRATION 10

Excited Friends Flowchart

"Who are the people in your (social sphere) that share our excitement/concern for (ministry/people)?"

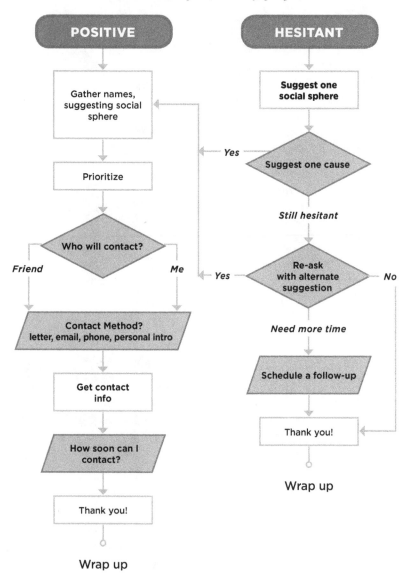

Go to top of
positive column

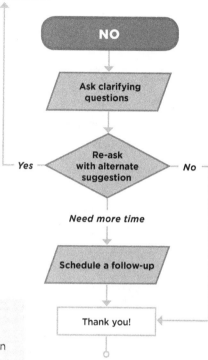

NO

Ask clarifying
questions

Re-ask
with alternate
suggestion

Yes

No

Need more time

Schedule a follow-up

Thank you!

Wrap up

YOU MUST:

1. **Ask** for excited friends in
   the appointment

2. Ask "**Who are**" not "Do
   you know?"

3. Who shares **excitement**
   for [ministry focus] or
   concern for [people
   group]

4. **Follow through**

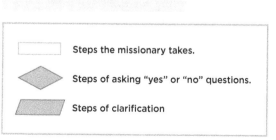

Steps the missionary takes.

Steps of asking "yes" or "no" questions.

Steps of clarification

ILLUSTRATION 11

Letter/Invitation for Hosted Small Group

Dear (name here),

I want to introduce you to a friend of mine, Sally Singer. I've known Sally for years—she grew up here in the Boston area, and we share a common heart and passion for Jesus.

Sally is a missionary with ABC Ministries in Dallas, Texas. ABC Ministries is a missions base committed to the Great Commission through worship, evangelism, Christian education, training, equipping young adults, being mindful of the poor, and doing other acts of justice. I've been a prayer and financial partner with Sally in ministry for over six years, and I have thoroughly enjoyed being connected with her. She is trustworthy, faithful, and encouraging to my life in the Lord!

I want to recommend Sally's ministry to you. I really think you would benefit from connecting with her as much as I have. Sally is going to be visiting Boston from October 26th through the 30th, and I'd love to introduce you to her. I will be hosting a cookout at my house on Saturday the 27th at 4:30pm, and I would love for you to come. It would give you a chance to meet Sally and get to know a little about her ministry.

I will be following up with you in a few days to verify your attendance. I look forward to speaking with you.

Blessings!

Steve

NOTES

Chapter 2: Living Beyond the Myths

1. Please keep in mind, when I talk about partnership development, I'm often talking about the whole process: raising support, the giver, the Church's role, lifestyle, the missionary's role, etc.—all of it.

Chapter 3: Biblical Stewardship

1. See also Haggai 2:8; Psalm 50:10–12; 24:1 (NET); 1 Chronicles 29:11; Job 41:11.

Chapter 5: Teamwork in the New Testament

1. Many missionaries are afraid that, if they talk to their friends, family, and people in their circles about money, it is going to ruin their relationships. I have done partnership since 2006; I have not lost one friend, but I have gained many more. As I have taught thousands of missionaries how to raise their own support through financial partnership teams, there have only been one or two missionaries who have told me that it hurt one or two relationships. Out of all the stories I have heard, 99 percent of the time I have not heard anything but positive that comes out of relationships around this issue of partnership. Paul had a great relationship with his team, I have a great relationship with my team, and you can have a great relationship with your team as well.

Chapter 6: Self-Funding vs. Partnership

1. See Leviticus 7:6, 8–10, 14, 28–36.

Chapter 7: Living By Faith Alone?

1. Ellinwood, Frank F. *Questions and Phases of Modern Missions,* Charleston, SC: Dodd, Mead and Company, BiblioBazaar, 2010, 146.

Chapter 10: Prepare for Contact

1. The quotation is attributed to Roger Maris on many inspirational quotation sites (see brainyquote.com/quotes/quotes/r/rogermaris/27401.html). Maris broke the Major League Baseball record for homeruns during the 1961 season, breaking Babe Ruth's single-season record.

Chapter 12: Share the Vision & Invite to Partner

1. In all the trainings I have conducted, with all the missionaries who have followed the model I have laid out in this book, and of all the people they have approached about financial partnership, about 35 percent become financial partners. When missionaries have done all their meetings by video chat, the number of partners drops to 8 percent.

BIBLIOGRAPHY

Alcorn, Randy C. *Money, Possessions, and Eternity.* Carol Stream: Tyndale House Publisher, 2003.

Barnett, Betty J. *Friend Raising: Building a Missionary Support Team That Lasts.* Seattle: YWAM Publishing, 2002.

Blomberg, Craig L. *Interpreting the Parables.* Downers Grove: InterVarsity Press, 2009.

Blomberg, Craig L. *Neither Poverty nor Riches: A Biblical Theology of Possessions (New Studies in Biblical Theology).* Downers Grove: InterVarsity Press, 2000.

Dillon, William P. *People Raising: A Practical Guide to Raising Support.* Chicago: Moody Press, 1993.

Johnson, Paul. *More Than Money More Than Faith: Successfully Raising Missionary Support in the Twenty-first Century.* Enumclaw, WA: Pleasant Word Publishing, 2007.

Morton, Scott. *Funding Your Ministry: Whether You're Gifted or Not.* Colorado Springs: Dawson Media, 1999.

Sommer, Pete. *Getting Sent: A Relational Approach to Support Raising.* Downers Grove: InterVarsity Press, 1999.

INTERNATIONAL HOUSE *of* PRAYER

••

24/7 LIVE WORSHIP AND PRAYER

ihopkc.org/prayerroom

••

Since September 19, 1999, we have continued in night-and-day prayer with worship as the foundation of our ministry to win the lost, heal the sick, and make disciples, as we labor alongside the larger Body of Christ to see the Great Commission fulfilled, and to function as forerunners who prepare the way for the return of Jesus.

By the grace of God, we are committed to combining 24/7 prayers for justice with 24/7 works of justice until the Lord returns. We believe we are better equipped to reach out to others when our lives are rooted in prayer that focuses on intimacy with God and intercession for breakthrough of the fullness of God's power and purpose for this generation.

The Best *of the* Prayer Room Live

SIX LIVE WORSHIP ALBUMS PER YEAR

••

Every other month we release a new volume of worship
and prayer recordings from our Global Prayer Room.

Subscribe today at **ihopkc.org/bestof**

International House of Prayer Missions Base, 3535 E. Red Bridge Road, Kansas City, MO 64137
(816) 763-0200 | info@ihopkc.org

INTERNATIONAL
HOUSE *of* PRAYER
U N I V E R S I T Y

··

ENCOUNTER GOD. DO HIS WORKS. CHANGE THE WORLD.

ihopkc.org/ihopu

··

International House of Prayer University (IHOPU) is a full-time Bible school which exists to equip this generation in the Word and in the power of the Holy Spirit for the bold proclamation of the Lord Jesus and His return.

As part of the International House of Prayer, our Bible school is built around the centrality of the Word and 24/7 prayer with worship, equipping students in the Word and the power of the Spirit for the bold proclamation of the Lord Jesus and His kingdom. Training at IHOPU forms not only minds but also lifestyle and character, to sustain students for a life of obedience, humility, and anointed service in the kingdom. Our curriculum combines in-depth biblical training with discipleship, practical service, outreach, and works of compassion.

IHOPU is for students who long to encounter Jesus. With schools of ministry, music, media, and missions, our one- to four-year certificate and diploma programs prepare students to engage in the Great Commission and obey Jesus' commandments to love God and people.

> "What Bible School has 'prayer' on its curriculum? The most important thing a man can study is the prayer part of the Book. But where is this taught?
>
> Let us strip off the last bandage and declare that many of our presidents and teachers do not pray, shed no tears, know no travail. Can they teach what they do not know?"
>
> –Leonard Ravenhill, *Why Revival Tarries*

International House of Prayer University, 12901 S. US Highway 71, Grandview, MO 64030
(816) 763-0243 | info@ihopu.org

International House *of* Prayer

INTERNSHIPS

INTRO TO IHOPKC • FIRE IN THE NIGHT
ONE THING INTERNSHIP • SIMEON COMPANY

ihopkc.org/internships

Internships exist to see people equipped with the Word of God, ministering in the power of the Holy Spirit, engaged in intercession, and committed to outreach and service.

Our four internships are three to six months long and accommodate all seasons of life. The purpose of the internships is to further prepare individuals of all ages as intercessors, worshipers, messengers, singers, and musicians for the work of the kingdom. While each internship has a distinctive age limit, length, and schedule, they all share the same central training components: corporate prayer and worship meetings, classroom instruction, practical ministry experience, outreach, and relationship-building.

Biblical teaching in all of the internships focuses on intimacy with Jesus, ministry in the power of the Holy Spirit, the forerunner ministry, evangelizing the lost, justice, and outreach. Interns also receive practical, hands-on training in the prophetic and healing ministries.

Upon successful completion of a six-month internship or two three-month tracks, some will stay and apply to join IHOPKC staff.

Our IHOPKC Leadership Team

Our leadership team of over a hundred and fifty men and women, with diversity of experience, background, and training, represents twenty countries and thirty denominations and oversees eighty-five departments on our missions base. With a breadth of experience in pastoral ministry, missions work, education, and the marketplace, this team's training in various disciplines includes over forty master's degrees and ten doctorates.

International House of Prayer Missions Base, 3535 E. Red Bridge Road, Kansas City, MO 64137
(816) 763-0200 | internships@ihopkc.org

MIKE BICKLE
TEACHING LIBRARY
—— *Free Teaching & Resource Library* ——

This International House of Prayer resource library, encompassing more than thirty years of Mike's teaching ministry, provides access to hundreds of resources in various formats, including streaming video, downloadable video, and audio, accompanied by study notes and transcripts, absolutely free of charge.

You will find some of Mike's most requested titles, including *The Gospel of Grace*; *The First Commandment*; *Jesus, Our Magnificent Obsession*; *Romans: Theology of Holy Passion*; *The Sermon on the Mount: The Kingdom Lifestyle*; and much more.

We encourage you to freely copy any of these teachings to share with others or use in any way: "our copyright is the right to copy." Older messages are being prepared and uploaded from Mike's teaching archives, and all new teachings are added immediately.

Visit mikebickle.org

International House of Prayer Missions Base, 3535 E. Red Bridge Road, Kansas City, MO 64137
(816) 763-0200 | info@ihopkc.org | ihopkc.org

International House *of* Prayer

INTERNSHIPS

INTRO TO IHOPKC • FIRE IN THE NIGHT
ONE THING INTERNSHIP • SIMEON COMPANY

ihopkc.org/internships

Internships exist to see people equipped with the Word of God, ministering in the power of the Holy Spirit, engaged in intercession, and committed to outreach and service.

Our four internships are three to six months long and accommodate all seasons of life. The purpose of the internships is to further prepare individuals of all ages as intercessors, worshipers, messengers, singers, and musicians for the work of the kingdom. While each internship has a distinctive age limit, length, and schedule, they all share the same central training components: corporate prayer and worship meetings, classroom instruction, practical ministry experience, outreach, and relationship-building.

Biblical teaching in all of the internships focuses on intimacy with Jesus, ministry in the power of the Holy Spirit, the forerunner ministry, evangelizing the lost, justice, and outreach. Interns also receive practical, hands-on training in the prophetic and healing ministries.

Upon successful completion of a six-month internship or two three-month tracks, some will stay and apply to join IHOPKC staff.

Our IHOPKC Leadership Team

Our leadership team of over a hundred and fifty men and women, with diversity of experience, background, and training, represents twenty countries and thirty denominations and oversees eighty-five departments on our missions base. With a breadth of experience in pastoral ministry, missions work, education, and the marketplace, this team's training in various disciplines includes over forty master's degrees and ten doctorates.

International House of Prayer Missions Base, 3535 E. Red Bridge Road, Kansas City, MO 64137
(816) 763-0200 | internships@ihopkc.org

MIKE BICKLE
TEACHING LIBRARY
—— *Free Teaching & Resource Library* ——

This International House of Prayer resource library, encompassing more than thirty years of Mike's teaching ministry, provides access to hundreds of resources in various formats, including streaming video, downloadable video, and audio, accompanied by study notes and transcripts, absolutely free of charge.

You will find some of Mike's most requested titles, including *The Gospel of Grace*; *The First Commandment*; *Jesus, Our Magnificent Obsession*; *Romans: Theology of Holy Passion*; *The Sermon on the Mount: The Kingdom Lifestyle*; and much more.

We encourage you to freely copy any of these teachings to share with others or use in any way: "our copyright is the right to copy." Older messages are being prepared and uploaded from Mike's teaching archives, and all new teachings are added immediately.

Visit mikebickle.org

International House of Prayer Missions Base, 3535 E. Red Bridge Road, Kansas City, MO 64137
(816) 763-0200 | info@ihopkc.org | ihopkc.org